D1450577

THE LITTLE BLACK BOOK OF BUSINESS STATISTICS

Michael C. Thomsett

American Management Association

This publication is designed to provide accurate and authoritative information in regard to the subject matter covered. It is sold with the understanding that the publisher is not engaged in rendering legal, accounting, or other professional service. If legal advice or other expert assistance is required, the services of a competent professional person should be sought.

Library of Congress Cataloging-in-Publication Data

Thomsett, Michael C.
   The little black book of business statistics / Michael C. Thomsett.
      p. cm.
   Includes index.
   ISBN 0-8144-7731-3
   1. Business forecasting.   2. Commercial statistics.   I. Title.
HD30.27.T57   1990   90-55214
658.4'0355'015195—dc20   CIP

© 1990 Michael C. Thomsett.
All rights reserved.
Printed in the United States of America.

This publication may not be reproduced,
stored in a retrieval system,
or transmitted in whole or in part,
in any form or by any means, electronic,
mechanical, photocopying, recording, or otherwise,
without the prior written permission of AMACOM,
a division of American Management Association,
135 West 50th Street, New York, NY 10020.

BOMC offers recordings and compact discs, cassettes
and records. For information and catalog write to
BOMR, Camp Hill, PA 17012.

Contents

Table of Symbols:
Statistical Symbols Used in This Book

X^2 chi-square

R coefficient of correlation

R^2 coefficient of determination

$\binom{a}{b}$ factorial expression

$n!$ factorial of value n

$\bar{x}$ mean (average)

n	number of values or unknown value
Pr	probability
$\sqrt{n}$	square root of n
σ	standard deviation

Introduction

Statistics are mendacious truths.

—Lionel Strachey

As a manager, you are expected to act as a corporate seer, an expert on what will happen in the future. You forecast, budget, and calculate risk for your company and communicate projections to decision makers. Your job, in fact, could be divided into two distinct ranges of effort. First is the maintenance function: summarizing past events and processing current information. Second is the less tangible and more difficult task aimed at estimating future events—the amount of money your department will spend, transactions that will be processed, or the level of sales a division will achieve.

Top management values the manager whose perceptions and observations of the past and present are applied to help make judgments about what may happen next week or next year. Management depends heavily on such information from informed sources, mainly from its own team of executives and managers.

Future profits, for example, may exist at the extremes (big profits or big losses). But there is a most likely range of outcomes you're likely to experience. If, through the use of statistics, you're able to evaluate an idea in terms of risk and probability, you will be perceived as a valuable member of the company team. A lot of effort goes into expressing opinions and estimating on the basis of a guess—although few would admit it. That's because what's often missing is a specific method for identifying probabilities.

1

This book presents many useful techniques to help you improve your abilities as a forecaster, to give you the "super vision" that managers desire and are expected to possess. There are many more advanced statistical techniques besides the ones covered here, but they do not offer value in solving the problems you're most likely to confront.

With the techniques presented in this book, you can improve your ability to answer the most difficult and challenging questions, even when a lot of variables are present and even when you hesitate to put yourself on the line with a prediction. You will feel more confident in expressing your opinion about a marketing idea, a new product, or a budget by knowing the odds and by testing samples to narrow down what will likely happen in the future.

How can you estimate future events with any degree of certainty when so many different outcomes are possible? And how can you express your estimates with confidence, given the chance that you will be wrong? These are the questions you must struggle with every day.

The answers are found in applying some of the basic techniques of statistical analysis. These principles do not magically transform estimates into concrete, definite answers, nor do they reduce the number of possible outcomes. They do provide you with the means for defining—both for yourself and for top management—how estimates are developed and how their dependability can be assessed and compared.

We often depend on historical information as the sole basis for estimating the future—if only because we don't have any other body of facts to begin with. You can begin with the past, though, and transform information, narrow it down, and arrive at some useful definitions in reporting the following:

1. The degree of dependability in the information used to make estimates
2. The most probable, or likely, outcomes
3. The risk level of making a decision based on your estimates

If you don't establish a set of rules estimating the future you may have severe difficulty in making a convincing case. Without those rules, your estimate is only an unsupported guess. To be able to stand behind your conclusion with confidence, you need to back up an estimate with reasonable assumptions that others will accept.

This is a problem, however, because no two people will always study a problem in the same way. Try this experiment: Give several people an identical series of facts about a problem and ask them to draw a conclusion. You will be amazed at the variety of different answers you receive. People are creative in their interpretations. They will perceive both the problem itself and the facts they receive in dissimilar ways. They also hold points of view that do not necessarily agree with yours. It is inaccurate to assume that a problem has one "right" solution, or that a question can have only one "right" answer. The spectrum of possible interpretations may be infinite. That's what makes people so interesting—each of us has our own approach to problems. But this same condition also adds to the challenge we all face in business, every day and every time we interact with someone else.

This is where a strong grounding in the use of statistics will help to clear the air. By approaching a problem from a scientific point of view, you will learn to isolate the applicable body of facts and then build a case that cannot be disputed by people with good motives but opposing points of view. This does not mean that you should manipulate the facts to produce the desired conclusion, but rather that an impartial evaluation of the available facts should lead you to a likely answer.

You must apply "facts" to situations, rather than use them inappropriately or merely assume that the same approach works in unlike situations. You may be frustrated in your attempts to estimate and project accurately, not because you lack skill, but because you do not select facts as carefully as you should. You are expected to project continually as part of your job. This is not a mathematical skill, but a judgmental one.

This book demonstrates how statistical information can be gathered, tested, and applied to solve problems managers face every day. Our approach is to introduce techniques and concepts of business statistics and demonstrate how they apply to situations you may face. It is not enough to work only with a method for using numbers; there must also be a context. We use many examples to demonstrate how a statistical technique applies to you. And each chapter concludes with a number of work project questions. Answers are provided in the Appendix.

Although the subject of this work is statistics, it is also much more. The use of statistics is introduced and explained in the context of developing a method for approaching and solving problems, making decisions, and conveying information to other people.

Business communication depends on the interpretation of values, selection of compiled numerical information, and anticipation of what is likely to occur in the future. Your challenge is to select the right facts needed to draw an accurate conclusion; to present your ideas to others in a concise and understandable format; and to simplify rather than complicate the decision-making process.

This Little Black Book explains the building blocks of business statistics. It is not a book of remote theories and ambiguous formulas, but a handbook that every manager can use to improve his or her abilities in interpretation and communication. You will master what at first may seem an intimidating body of symbols, formulas, and obscure ideas and learn how to use mathematical techniques on the job.

Statistics often are viewed with suspicion. We all know that, depending on how numbers are manipulated, different conclusions can be drawn from the same facts. We propose that responsible and properly documented use of statistics will help reduce this all-too-common problem. You have probably heard others quote statistics in business meetings or discussions. It's a dangerous but convenient habit to support points of view with statistical statements such as:

"Studies have shown that. . . ."
"Ninety-five percent of all employees. . . ."
"There's a three-to-one probability that. . . ."

Avoid making undocumented statements quoting statistical sources. Set a goal for yourself that whenever you refer to a statistical conclusion, you will have a source at hand that's both accurate and relevant. If you refer to studies, be sure those studies support your contention. When offering an argument with the use of percentages, first check your facts. And when discussing probabilities, first be sure you have an accurate conclusion. You should apply a high standard to yourself, expecting that your statistical information will be questioned or challenged. Thus, you ensure that information you share with others is accurate and can be backed up with the applicable facts.

Think of this Little Black Book as your ultimate weapon, to be used in the war against informational loose ends. Then, when your conclusions are challenged in a meeting, you will be able to refer to the documentation in the back of your report, confidently establishing your professionalism. Then, back in your department, be sure to check the drawer where you keep this book to make sure your secret weapon is still there.

1
Statistics in Business

The greatest American superstition is belief in facts.

—Hermann A. Keyserling

The president always led off meetings with a dizzying array of projections. Future sales would skyrocket, profits would grow, and the company would soon be a national success story. A new manager, impressed with the apparent growth potential for the company, asked one veteran executive how accurate the president's statistics were. The executive replied, "Drop a few zeros off the sales figures and put a negative sign in front of the profit projection—and you'll get a pretty good idea of where we're going."

The volume of data you must confront every day makes a consistently detailed analysis impractical. Thus, the use of statistical techniques is a necessity. By evaluating a selective, isolated grouping of information or by dealing in averages, you can assign significance, discover trends, and project likely future events.

Statistics as a mathematical discipline suffers from a negative reputation, largely because statistical concepts often are misused or used so selectively that information is distorted rather than clarified. By carefully setting rules for yourself, however, you will be able to use the techniques of statistics to improve communication and to support the recommendations you convey to others.

You are expected to develop reliable information in three major areas where statistical techniques can be put to work:

1. *Forecasting and budgeting.* All managers are involved in the budgeting process in one way or another. You may prepare the annual budget for your company, your department, or for a special project; a factory supervisor forecasts output and defect levels; and a processing department manager forecasts the number of transactions to be processed, number of employees needed to complete the task, and expenses involved in accomplishing the task.

2. *Market testing.* New products are tested by manufacturing companies in regional trials; services may be tested and costed out in the same way. But even if you are not directly involved in selling your company's product or service, you still need to apply the estimating skills used to test-market—even if only for an idea. You may recommend a change in procedures, for example; in order to gain approval, you will have to "sell" the idea to the decision maker. Your task will be to prove that profits will increase as the result of putting your information into action.

3. *Risk analysis.* Your company's top management is always aware of risk. Marketing a new product, hiring a new employee, computerizing, and investing in long-term assets are all forms of risk. Accepting your ideas also represents risk—if your idea does not produce profits, then the company will lose money. Statistical techniques that identify risk levels help decision makers to identify how much risk is appropriate and whether or not a specific action is worth that risk.

DEFINING STATISTICS

Statistics may be defined in two ways. First, it is a collection of numerical information from which conclusions may be drawn. And second, it is a mathematical process of analysis.

Example: A year's profit picture is analyzed by division, divided into quarters, and compared with previous periods, all for the purpose of judging the company's performance. In this respect, the **statistics** are the collective numerical values with which you work.

Example: A coming year's budget is prepared after a study of trends in each classification of cost and expense. Some accounts are estimated on the basis of percentage increases, others on per-employee use or historical trends. In this respect, **statistics** refers to the process of analyzing and using the numerical information you have collected.

---

statistics—(1) a body of numerical information.
(2) a form of mathematics that involves the analysis of numerical information.

In many applications, it is impossible to study a complete array of available information. You will have to take a sample for testing purposes; or you will have to deal only with averages, because a series of possible events cannot be easily reduced to a forecast.

Example: An auditor has the task of ensuring that a company's disbursements have been recorded accurately. The company issues over ten thousand checks per year, and examining each one would be expensive and time-consuming. Thus, the auditor selects a random sample.

Example: A plant manager is attempting to reduce the frequency of defects each shift experiences. The volume of manufacturing activity is high; thus, a detailed study of causes is not practical. The manager selects a sample crew on each shift and analyzes the defect rate in an attempt to isolate causes.

In both these cases, the purpose of selecting a sample is to identify (1) the approximate degree of inaccuracy or (2) the cause of a recurring problem. The entire body of information (a year's checks or the number of units manufactured) is referred to as a **population;** the smaller grouping of study is called a **sample.**

----

population—the complete body of information, facts, or numbers to be subjected to statistical study.

sample—a small part of the population, selected for study and believed to represent the attributes of the population.

Use of samples is the basic idea underlying statistics. In a business meeting, it would not be possible to convey information concerning a large population of data; we must communicate in terms of samples. Anyone who has discussed financial information in a meeting has already applied this technique.

Example: An accountant presents a report to the president that describes buying patterns of customers. The report includes average amount of purchase, age and economic status of the typical customer, and response to specific products. All this information is based on surveys of relatively small groups or on averages of a large body of information. It would not have been practical for the accountant to prepare a report summarizing every sale and every customer's attributes. In addition, such a detailed report would not have provided the type of information the president needed in order to draw an informed conclusion.

The most difficult step for most people who confront a large information base is deciding what information is relevant, how to arrange it, and how to draw conclusions. It might seem at first glance that the biggest difficulty is finding the information itself. But, problems are solved not only by gathering facts, but by selecting the right facts and knowing how to convert them into something meaningful and conclusive.

Statistical skill—restricted to the manipulation of numbers—is only the vehicle you use in deriving a solution. Before you can proceed to the actual study, you must first understand the nature of the task. This is why a purely academic approach is useless; of greater value is your experience on the front lines of corporate problem solving.

Example: A marketing manager has been given the task of estimating the average dollar volume that each salesperson will generate next year.

This information will be used for the development of assumptions as part of an income forecast. The manager knows from experience that newly recruited salespeople will not produce the same volume of sales as more experienced individuals. Thus, the estimate must be broken down into segments:

1. A study of the average dollar volume produced during the first year a salesperson is hired
2. An estimate of the average dollar volume produced by salespeople who have been on the job between one and three years
3. An estimate of average dollar volume produced by salespeople with more than three years on the job

These samples must be based on estimates of the number of new salespeople per month expected in the coming year, which in turn must be based on historical averages and current recruitment goals. The samples must also be modified by an estimate of the number of salespeople in each classification who are expected to resign, again based on the averages experienced in the past.

Several statistical techniques will be used in this example: The manager will use samples to develop average volume in each group; those averages will be increased or reduced according to an average of previous years' hiring and terminations; and the final results will be used to develop a sales forecast for the entire company.

In this case, a simple average would not be accurate, nor could it be used to judge the accuracy of the statistical study. For example, if actual recruitment fell below expected levels, the estimated volume for first-year salespeople would be off. And if terminations among salespeople with higher-than-average dollar volume were higher or lower than previous years' averages, that too would throw off the sales forecast.

The purpose of statistical studies, such as those performed for every estimate of future financial results, is not to isolate and conclusively decide what *will* occur. Rather, it is to report the likely results as accurately and as scientifically as possible. Every business decision must be based on assumptions of risk and reward; thus, the use of samples must be as accurate and consistent as possible.

APPLYING STATISTICAL INFORMATION

In coming chapters, you will see how certain techniques can be used to summarize information and draw conclusions about likely future events. An example of this is isolating average dollar volume produced by each salesperson in each classification by years of service. This form of statistics involves the methods of summarizing a group of related absolute values and is referred to as **descriptive statistics.**

Beyond the techniques for summarizing and studying absolute values is **statistical inference,** which is a conclusion drawn by studying a small sample. The best-known example of this is an opinion poll or survey, in which a very small group is questioned and a generalized conclusion is derived to represent a much larger population.

----

descriptive statistics—methods of studying and summarizing a series of numbers.

statistical inference—the isolated study of a small sample, used to draw conclusions about a larger population.

Whenever you approach a task, the first step must be to gather the right information. So many of the errors made in business derive from the failure to take this first step. For example, a problem is posed and the solution is based on a series of facts that simply don't address the problem. The proper use of statistics must be based on a careful selection and organization of the facts you will use.

Three methods for reporting numerical information in response to a question or to solve a problem are: gathering facts, arranging facts, and clarifying the question being asked.

1. *Gathering facts.* In some cases, the mere accumulation of the right data will solve the problem. For example, the president of the company wants to know how much money was spent on salaries last year; or the accounting department assigns rent on the basis of square footage for each section.

2. *Arranging facts.* Beyond gathering the right facts, the arrangement of information may also answer someone else's question. A sales manager, asked to prepare a report showing the most productive and least productive salespeople, need only arrange information in the order of volume.

3. *Clarifying the question.* The gathering and arrangement of facts to give to someone else is a basic, although common, form of reporting. But in most instances, the request is made for a purpose beyond the mere conveyance of information. By asking what information the other person wants, you will be able to provide more than raw data. That's where the combination of statistical techniques and your own insight will improve your management and reporting skills.

Example: A word processing department manager was asked to prepare a report summarizing turnaround time for documents of various lengths. She asked for clarification and discovered the purpose of the request. Management was considering upgrading the current system and replacing it with one believed to be more efficient. With the problem clearly understood, the manager was able to provide the information needed— a report of the *changes* in turnaround time that occurred as the volume of work increased.

Example: The president of a marketing company was considering expanding into a new territory. He hired a consultant to study the likely demand for the company's product. Because the president did not limit the scope of the report, it was expensive and largely useless. All the president had really needed was a summary of population trends and competitive factors. Chances are, the information could have been obtained with a call to an area's library or chamber of commerce.

ACCURACY IN SAMPLES

If you attempt to study an entire population and its size is too large for timely and accurate reporting, your approach will lack the efficiency that sample studies provide. Many populations (including the number of transactions occurring in a large company, units of production, or the number of customers you serve) are too diverse and too large for detailed study; thus, the use of a representative sample is a logical and time-saving alternative.

Entire populations cannot always be studied, not only because they are large, but because the purpose itself might not be served by a thorough analysis. For example, a plant manager wants to determine how long employees can work without the rate of defects increasing. If one shift produces 20,000 units per hour, it would be very expensive to work that shift for many hours without pause to find the point at which defect rates begin to rise. Similarly, a stress test applied to a sample of products would indicate the point of breakage; it would serve no purpose to apply that test to every unit manufactured.

Although it is not necessary to test entire populations, the sample must be broad enough to be fair and accurate. A key criterion in using an isolated sample is: THE SAMPLE MUST FAIRLY REPRESENT THE POPULATION. Although this point may seem obvious, it is often ignored in sample testing. A manager may select a sample likely to help draw a predetermined conclusion—even on an unconscious level. Thus, the proper use of sampling techniques must also involve an impartial mechanism for selection.

Example: An auditor wants to select a sample of disbursements over the past year. The first approach is to pick 200 checks from a population of 10,000; however, the auditor picks each one by hand and unintentionally concentrates on only one type of disbursement. It does not necessarily reflect the error rate of the population. As an alternative, the range of check numbers is isolated, and 200 are selected at random.

Example: A customer service manager wants to study the response time to customer requests. She first makes the selection according to the type of call; however, this approach is flawed, because response times vary by complexity of request. The sample is revised to study every twentieth call received.

Example: A company conducts a survey of existing customers to determine whether a new product will find acceptance. The first sample, however, is of customers who buy from the company regularly. Management realizes that this is not representative of the "typical" or "average" customer and conducts another survey at random that is not limited to a particular type of customer.

In the last example, the flaw is obvious. It might be that repeat customers were selected in the belief that they would be most likely to respond to a survey. But that very selection made the sample unrepresentative. For the sample to be fair, it must be selected for the right reasons, and not for the purpose of increasing response or affecting the sample's outcome.

A sample cannot be expected to produce accurate results if conditions have changed since the sample information was gathered. This is a critical point, and one that is often forgotten by those who depend too heavily on statistical information without a corresponding review of the nonstatistical facts and conditions.

Example: A manager conducts a statistical study to determine how quickly newly hired employees are trained to perform their jobs. He studies a sample of employees hired last year. However, overlooked in this study is the fact that new training techniques have been put into place since those employees were hired.

We cannot always know for certain that a particular sample will be truly representative of the population, even when that sample is taken at random and current conditions are identical to the time that the sample was taken. However, random sampling does remove all preconditions and assumptions that may be present with other methods. An auditor may unconsciously select only the largest transactions; or the customer service manager may believe that a certain type of request is representative when, in fact, it is not. Even with an attempt to achieve objectivity, a poorly drawn sample will mislead and cause an inaccurate result.

THE PROBABILITY FACTOR

The reliability of a sample can be estimated with reasonable certainty under the rules of probability. In a sense, probability is the mathematical opposite of statistics: A probability is the study of results when a process is well understood; a statistic shows us the result when we're not sure how the process occurs.

Example: If you flip a coin 100 times, heads is likely to come up 50 times. We understand that the chance is 50-50. The process is understood.

Example: A review of 100 coin flips shows that in one instance heads came up 53 times; in another, it came up 49 times; and in a third test, heads appeared 48 times. From these results, it may be statistically concluded that, on average, heads appears half the time. From this information, the future number of heads can be estimated statistically, even if we do not understand the process that determines the result.

You use probability estimates to judge the risk in a decision or to protect against the chance of a future loss. Even if the loss is unlikely to occur statistically, probability may demand protection.

Example: Your company owns a warehouse and stores its inventory there. The total value of the facility and goods exceeds $12 million. With the science of probability, your insurance company can tell you that a fire or other loss will occur in one of every 10,000 warehouses; thus, your chances of suffering a loss are very low. However, your company could not afford a loss of that magnitude, so it purchases insurance and pays premiums to protect its assets. Statistically, companies that install sprinkler systems suffer fewer losses than those that do not. So, your company is able to reduce its insurance costs by installing sprinklers.

In this case, probability and statistics both apply. First is the remote probability of a catastrophe—one that is unlikely to occur but that would represent a serious loss of value. Second is the statistical fact that risk—to the company and to the insurer—is drastically reduced with safety measures.

In future chapters, the principles of probability are expanded and shown in situations you will face as a manager. In the evaluation of business risk in many forms, probability and statistics are closely related ideas.

Using the concepts of statistical inference—carefully selecting a representative sample of a larger population—will help reduce the analysis of any task to a manageable level. And as long as you select a sample on an impartial basis, the *probability* that it is representative will increase. Thus, the basic principles of probability can be applied to the very process you use in approaching a large-population problem and in developing a statistical base for study.

This idea is best demonstrated by referring again to the example of insuring business assets. The insurance company sets its premium rates according to historical incidents of loss. The premium charged to each policyholder must be adequate to cover the expected losses of the *population* of businesses with warehouses, as well as the insurer's own overhead and profit requirements. As statistical information changes, premiums are adjusted to reflect newer, updated information.

At any given time, the probability of a loss must be calculated on the likely rate of loss. However, the statistical information available to the actuaries setting rates constantly changes those rates. If more losses occur with certain types of properties, materials, or locations, that statistical information must be incorporated into the probability study. And if, by taking safety measures, a company reduces its exposure to loss, the rates may be reduced.

TEN RULES FOR KEEPING IT SIMPLE

A comprehension of statistics and probabilities need not be complicated. As abstract mathematical ideas, the formulas and equations are intimidating and, for a good number of managers, difficult to master. However, when those same principles are applied to situations with which you are familiar, the building blocks are already in place. All that's required is to apply the techniques to solving problems you already face.

Follow these important rules as you read this book to help you learn how to apply statistical skills in your job:

1. Master each term or expression as it's introduced. Terminology in statistics is, by necessity, highly specialized.
2. Use the Table of Symbols at the front of this book as a quick reference to statistical symbols and their meaning. We explain

these as they are introduced and provide examples with each formula.

3. Test each idea as it's introduced. Answer the questions posed at the end of each chapter in the Work Project and check your work against the answers provided in the Appendix.

4. Be constantly aware that the mathematical techniques presented are the means toward solutions, and not the end result. You must continue to apply the judgment you already use in managing your department and use statistical techniques as one of many tools.

5. Review material from time to time, and refresh your memory and comprehension of principles. Sharpen your skills by applying techniques on the job whenever possible.

6. Do not skip material you think will not be of immediate interest. As with all forms of math, the information presented in one chapter is necessary to proceed to the next one.

7. No matter how complex or abstract an idea may seem at first, remember that there are only four basic math functions—addition, subtraction, multiplication, and division. Every formula and concept introduced in this book involves only these routines.

8. If you are having trouble grasping an idea, carefully read the examples in the section where it is introduced. The purpose of examples is to keep the discussion on familiar ground. Also, review all definitions as they are introduced in the context of the examples provided.

9. Keep notes of key formulas, definitions, and techniques. Although these are cross-referenced throughout the book, you may find it helpful to refer to your own notes as well.

10. Do not proceed to a new chapter until you are completely confident that you have mastered the material in the chapter you have just finished.

By following these guidelines, you will gain confidence and skill in applying statistical methods, in choosing appropriate samples from larger populations, and in combining the techniques of statistics and probability to aid in the decision-making process.

If you are involved in a "number-intensive" department such as accounting or auditing, the use of automated programs can help you manage a volume of information, as well as help you apply statistical skills. However, most managers deal with numbers only when preparing reports or budgets, so they cannot justify an investment in highly specialized software for statistical analysis. You can perform most of the mathematical routines introduced by using a hand calculator.

SETTING OBJECTIVES

Some people assume that statistics is too complex for anyone to grasp unless they have studied higher math in college. Some elements of statistics and probability are so abstract that a grounding in calculus is necessary; however, that advanced skill level is not required for the business applications you will put to use.

The use of Greek symbols to represent complex mathematical concepts and the appearance of lengthy formulas will undoubtedly intimidate many people and prevent them from attacking a text of statistics. However, by following a methodical approach and remembering the actual applications as they affect you in your daily tasks, you will not have difficulty in mastering business statistics.

Set goals for yourself on two levels. First, decide that you will master the basic skills, terminology, and formulas related to business statistics. Second, consider the following goals for use of statistical information in your job:

1. Validate every fact and series of facts you use in statistical claims and conclusions. Draw a clear reference between the answer to a problem and the assumption base used to arrive at it.

2. Be prepared to support your contentions with your assumption base. Don't just assume that someone else will agree with you; examine alternatives, and either propose alternative methods for approaching a solution or dismiss them as flawed by preparing and presenting proof in support of your position.

3. Never quote statistics that you cannot find and establish. Avoid

the habit of deferring to statistical statements to strengthen an argument and recognize that this habit only weakens credibility.

4. For every concept and technique involving statistics, find *appropriate* business applications and apply your skill in using those methods that work to solve problems you face. Avoid "over-statistifying" reports.

5. Avoid all arbitrary guesswork when dealing with financial information. In too many cases, projections are based on poorly supported assumptions, or on no assumptions whatsoever. Question budgets based on the previous year's levels, sales forecasts that assume percentage increases over the previous year, and similar practices. Always look for the statistical means for supporting projections.

6. Remember that every decision you make will affect someone else. Even in a highly automated, efficiently run, technological environment, the two-dimensional nature of statistical information must not be allowed to take priority over the human element. Use statistics as a tool, not as a replacement for sound decisions.

In Chapter 2, the basics of descriptive statistics are introduced and explained, along with examples and illustrations of their business applications.

WORK PROJECT

1. A sales manager wants to determine how long it takes to train newly recruited salespeople to the point that they are able to meet a monthly sales quota. Last year, 64 new people were hired. The manager studies a group of 8, and from that study develops a conclusion about the time required to train the typical new recruit.
   a. What statistical name describes the small group selected for the study?
   b. What statistical name describes the 64 newly hired people last year?
   c. Is this study accurate if new training procedures were installed at the beginning of this year?

2. Describe the three approaches for reporting numerical information listed below and describe how your experience as a manager will help you to improve your response:
   a. Gathering and conveying facts
   b. Arranging facts in a specific order
   c. Asking for clarification of what's needed
3. Flipping a coin 100 times will produce a number of heads and a number of tails. Explain how this process involves principles of statistics *and* probability.

2
Descriptive Statistics

As a rule we disbelieve all facts and theories for which we have no use.

—William James

> *"This used to be a profitable company," the president complained. "But we've lost money for the last three years. What do I tell the stockholders?"*
>
> *"Well," one executive piped up, "it's true that our three-year average is poor. But why cite performance? Let's blame it on statistics."*

You've been given an assignment that will involve reporting on trends in your department. You will have to summarize the numbers and explain what they mean, and although the task is complicated, you'll be given only five minutes to present your facts.

This is typical of the problems you face every day. With a huge amount of information available, you need to quickly identify the significance behind a group of numbers, tell other people what those numbers mean, and achieve these goals without the luxury of time.

Much of the work you do in communicating with others involves descriptive statistics—methods of studying and summarizing a series of numbers. Not only do you need to summarize the meaning of today's numbers, you also need to relate the information as part of a trend. Are the numbers better or worse than they were last month or last year? And what is likely to happen in the future?

Even more challenging is the need to tell others how predictable your estimates are. For example, you must project financial information for the coming year. Are your estimates fairly certain, or are they more difficult to pin down? The degree of predictability can be defined and compared by use of statistical techniques.

The process of estimating and defining begins with the collection of the numbers you will use. For example, to study trends in sales by division, you need to gather sales figures. To report on the cost of hiring new employees, you will start with information on salaries and benefits. And to study production trends, you will first gather records of shift performance for a period of weeks, months, or years.

DESCRIPTIVE STATISTICS TERMS

A collection of numbers that have not yet been summarized or interpreted is called **raw data.** It's not enough in most cases to simply report the raw data. The numbers in the list have to be summarized and explained.

Example: Your department will be automated during the next six months. You are asked for a summary of the number of transactions processed during the last six months, as well as the number you expect to process during the coming year. Your study produces the following summary of transactions.

Jan	3,301	Apr	3,109
Feb	3,419	May	3,611
Mar	2,880	Jun	3,598

Your raw data for this report consist of the number of transactions processed in each of the six months. A list of numbers is also described as a **distribution** of raw data. For example, when you're dealing with only six values, the distribution is fairly small. But when your raw data list involves 150 values, distribution is relatively large.

A distribution may involve values close to one another or far apart. For example, the six months' transactions above contain values between

2,880 and 3,611. This is the **range** of the distribution. Considering that the range is fairly consistent over the six months, a projection of future transaction volume will be fairly easy to calculate. But if the range were significantly larger, a dependable projection would be more difficult to calculate.

Example: Another processing department is given the same assignment: to report on transactions for the last six months and to estimate the same information for the coming year. However, that department's range is much larger than yours:

Jan	6,802	Apr	274
Feb	1,523	May	1,884
Mar	4,569	Jun	5,203

The range in this department is substantially greater than in the first case. So, calculating the likely number of transactions during the coming year will be more difficult, and the estimate will prove to be less dependable.

In comparing the tasks that you and the other manager face, you can describe the relative difficulty of making a projection by using the terms introduced to this point. For example, it would be fair to say, "Both departments begin by collecting raw data for the six-month period. The distribution in each case involves counting total transactions in each of six months. One department's calculations will be fairly dependable because the range is small; the other's will be less dependable because the range is large."

----

raw data—a list of related numbers that have not yet been summarized or interpreted.

distribution—a list of raw data that can involve a small number of values or a large number of values.

range—the difference in value between the smallest and the largest values in a distribution.

In presenting your report, you will want to treat the raw data in some way. Because the numbers by themselves do not reveal much, you should identify their **central tendency** through one of three statistics—mean, median, or mode. The purpose of a central tendency calculation is to summarize raw data so that they can be reported and given significance.

Example: You know the number of transactions processed in your department over the last six months. From this, you now want to estimate the likely number of transactions that will occur during the coming year. You need to identify the central tendency.

----

central tendency—a summary of raw data calculated to identify a significant trend or tendency in a distribution.

CALCULATING THE MEAN

Of the three central tendencies (mean, median, and mode), the best known is the **mean,** more popularly called the **average.** A mean is calculated by adding up the values in the distribution and then dividing the total by the number of values.

----

mean—the average of distribution, calculated by adding all the values and dividing that total by the number of values.

Example: The six-month summary of transactions has six values. To find the mean (average), add the six values and then divide by 6:

$$\frac{3,301 + 3,419 + 2,880 + 3,109 + 3,611 + 3,598}{6} = 3,320$$

The formula for calculating the mean can be summarized with the use of letters, also called summation notation. The symbol x represents a value, and *n* represents a number of values. A subscripted number following *x* is used to represent each value in a distribution. And when a line is placed above *x,* that stands for *average.* The formula for the mean is shown in Figure 2-1.

This formula is the same as the calculation shown above for the known six months' transactions. Your report could conclude that, based on the mean of six months, the coming year's transactions will be 3,320 per month. In practice, however, seasonal variation, growth trends, and other internal changes could make this simple projection inaccurate. For this reason, you may want to use one of several other averages that take into account such variables.

One of these is the simple **moving average.** This calculation stabilizes the range when the individual values vary considerably, or when you believe that averages are changing over time and you need to project how that trend will affect the future.

A moving average is appropriate when your distribution involves a time study such as monthly transactions. The moving average is calculated by (1) figuring the mean for a limited number of values, (2) adding one new value and dropping one old value for the next calculation, and (3) repeating this procedure through the entire distribution.

Example: You decide to report the six months of transactions in your department by a moving average. Using a series of three-month moving averages by calculating months one through three, two through four,

Figure 2-1.   Mean.

$$\bar{x} = \frac{x_1 + x_2 + x_3 + \cdots + x_n}{n}$$

$\bar{x} =$ mean (average)

$x =$ value

$n =$ number of values

three through five, and four through six, you will produce a moving average:

Month   Amount

Jan   3,301
Feb   3,419   } 3,200
Mar   2,880   }   } 3,136
Apr   3,109   }   }   } 3,200
May   3,611   }   }   }   } 3,439
Jun   3,598   }   }   }   }

The four calculations are summarized as follows:

Jan, Feb, Mar

$$\frac{3,301 + 3,419 + 2,880}{3} = 3,200$$

Feb, Mar, Apr

$$\frac{3,419 + 2,880 + 3,109}{3} = 3,136$$

Mar, Apr, May

$$\frac{2,880 + 3,109 + 3,611}{3} = 3,200$$

Apr, May, Jun

$$\frac{3,109 + 3,611 + 3,598}{3} = 3,439$$

Because the time span of this study is so short, an immediate trend cannot be dependably drawn. If the study covered a much longer period of time, a trend would be visible.

----

moving average—a series of calculations used to spot trends that develop over time. This technique offsets the effect of a widely varying range by identifying the *typical* past experience and *likely* future experience.

The moving average helps even out a trend, even when the distribution has a very wide range. Still, it's sometimes necessary to add more weight to some of the values on your distribution list.

CALCULATING THE WEIGHTED AVERAGE

By assigning differences in weight to one or more of the values in the distribution, the average is altered. This will give a more accurate average in some instances, such as when the latest information is more significant than earlier information or when seasonal changes make a distribution inaccurate without weighting.

----

weighted average—a method for computing an average in which greater weight is assigned to one or more of the values in the distribution.

Depending on the nature of the information in a distribution, one of several weighting methods can be used. One form of weighting is to increase the weight value for each subsequent period. Under this method, you assume that the latest information is more relevant than earlier information. Thus, the first value would have a weight of one; the second, two; and so forth. In a six-value distribution, the sixth value would be assigned a weight of six. To determine the average, the total is divided by the sum of the weights.

Example: Your six-month transaction summary is calculated on a **weighted-average** basis. You assume that the most recent month should have the greatest weight. Thus, you increase the weight of each subsequent value in the distribution:

Month	Amount		Weight		Total
Jan	3,301	×	1	=	3,301
Feb	3,419	×	2	=	6,838

Month	Amount		Weight		Total
Mar	2,880	×	3	=	8,640
Apr	3,109	×	4	=	12,436
May	3,611	×	5	=	18,055
Jun	3,598	×	6	=	21,588
Total			21		70,858

To calculate the average in this example, the sum of the weighted values is divided by the sum of the weights:

$$\frac{70,858}{21} = 3,374$$

Compare the weighted average of 3,374 to the simple average of 3,320. Because the largest value in the range is found in the later months and the smallest value occurs in the earlier months, the weighted average is higher than the simple average.

Variations of the weighted average are also possible. For example, you may decide to give equal weight to each value except the latest, which you double. In this case, you would divide the total by 7 (the first five months' values, plus 2 for the last month):

Month	Amount		Weight		Total
Jan	3,301	×	1	=	3,301
Feb	3,419	×	1	=	3,419
Mar	2,880	×	1	=	2,880
Apr	3,109	×	1	=	3,109
May	3,611	×	1	=	3,611
Jun	3,598	×	2	=	7,196
Total			7		23,516

To compute the average, divide the sum of the weighted values by the sum of the weights:

$$\frac{23,516}{7} = 3,359$$

The weighted-average technique can be applied to seasonally heavy periods instead of the latest period; and the moving averge can be combined with weighting so that you can spot trends. As these techniques are used for larger distributions and time periods, the calculations become more complex; thus, a shortcut is needed.

Example: When you submit your six-month transaction summary, management asks you to expand your report to include a weighted moving average for the last three years. What was a fairly simple series of calculations now becomes a time-consuming exercise.

The solution is to calculate the **exponential moving average.** With this method, an exponent is calculated and used as a multiplier, and changes in the moving average are added to or subtracted from the previous average. This method adds weight to the latest values and provides a simplified calculation for a large distribution. The larger the number of periods, the easier it is to compute average by the exponential method.

----

exponential moving average—a method for calculating the moving average for a large distribution or a large number of periods.

To compute the exponent, divide 2 by the number of values in the moving average. This produces the factor needed to properly compute the desired results.

Example: You want to calculate the moving average for 36 months of transactions (July through June for three years). You will compute the moving average in seven-month segments and want the latest information to be weighted. The total number of values in each calculation will be 7 (1 for each of the seven months).

Another point: The longer the averaging period, the better and easier it is to do exponential average. To calculate the exponent, divide 2 by 7 and round to two decimal places:

$$\frac{2}{7} = 0.29$$

Because your moving average will cover a 36-month period, use of the exponent will enable you to avoid a lot of math. To show how the exponential moving average is calculated, we will calculate the moving average for the first three seven-month periods. To perform this calculation, we need values for nine months:

Month	Number
Jul	2,167
Aug	1,943
Sep	2,005
Oct	2,299
Nov	1,976
Dec	2,286
Jan	2,314
Feb	2,295
Mar	2,363

We need to calculate the moving average for seven-month periods. The first will be July through January, followed by August through February, and then September through March.

1. Add the values for the first seven months:

Month	Number
Jul	2,167
Aug	1,943
Sep	2,005
Oct	2,299
Nov	1,976
Dec	2,286
Jan	2,314
Total	14,990

2. Calculate the average for the first seven months:

$$\frac{14,990}{7} = 2,141$$

3. Subtract the seven-month average from the eighth month's value:

February	2,295
Less	2,141 (average)
Remainder	154

4. Multiply the remainder by the exponent and round to the closest whole number:

$$154 \times 0.29 = 45$$

5. Add the calculated amount to the previous moving average:

Calculated	45
Previous average	2,141
Total	2,186

This process is repeated for each subsequent month. For the September-to-March calculation:

1. Isolate the difference:

March	2,363
Less	2,186 (average)
Remainder	177

2. Multiply by the exponent:

$$177 \times 0.29 = 51$$

3. Add to the previous average:

Calculated	51
Previous average	2,186
Total	2,237

At this point, the first three months' moving averages are complete:

Through	*Average*
Jan	2,141
Feb	2,186
Mar	2,237

When the newest month in the moving average has a value lower than the previous average, the remainder will be a negative value. In that instance, the product of the remainder and the exponent is subtracted from the previous average to calculate the latest month's average.

CALCULATING THE MEDIAN

The mean (or, average) is a common form of statistical work in business. But it does not always give you the exact information you need. In some cases, exceptionally large or small values in your distribution will skew the average to the point that it is not meaningful.

The **median** presents an alternative. The median is the exact middle value in a distribution; half the values are greater and half are less than the median. (See Figure 2-2.)

----

median—the middle value in a distribution, so that one-half of the values are greater and one-half are less.

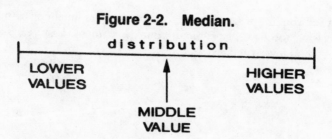

Figure 2-2. Median.

Going back to the first example of six months' transactions in your department at the beginning of this chapter, you can calculate the median by first listing the distribution in value order. (This can be done either in ascending or descending order.)

1. 3,611
2. 3,598
3. 3,419
4. 3,301
5. 3,109
6. 2,880

Because the list contains an even number of values, the exact middle is between the third and fourth values. The median is found by calculating the average of these values:

$$\frac{3,419 + 3,301}{2} = 3,360$$

Finding the median for a distribution with an odd number of values is easier. For example, the median for a distribution of seven values is the fourth value; and with nine values, it's the fifth value.

In some instances, the median will give you a more accurate central tendency than the mean (average) will. The average is most useful when your task is to spot growing trends over time. The median may be used when you want to find out what the representative middle number for a distribution is.

Example: You are preparing a report for the personnel department on absenteeism. You have 11 people in your department. Last year's absenteeism by employee (in days) was:

Employee	Days
1	57
2	11
3	9
4	9
5	6
6	4
7	4
8	3
9	2
10	1
11	0

The median is the sixth (middle) value, or 4. This is closer to the true representative absenteeism you can expect in a year, because one employee was absent last year for an unusually high number of days. The average in this example is 9.6 days, or twice the median.

The difference in the two calculations does not mean that one is more accurate in every case. The median, in this example, tells you the annual number of absent days you are *likely* to experience per employee. The facts tell us that the average during the last year was much greater.

Calculating the mean (average) and median is fairly simple. Your real challenge is deciding which to report and how to interpret your results. And that depends on the conclusions you want to reach. For example, your report may state that, on average, your department experienced 9.6 days of absenteeism per employee, but that in the coming year you expect each employee to be gone for 4 days per year. Your conclusion is supported by summarizing the average as well as the median, with explanations for the extraordinary circumstances in one case.

The median is also a telling statistic when you want to summarize a large body of information that is full of exceptions. For example, you are working on an analysis of the average dollar amount of sale by customer. A computer printout lists all sales last year, arranged in ascending dollar value. Some sales were in the thousands of dollars, and some were less than one dollar. But the majority were between $30 and $40 per customer. If the purpose of your study is to forecast future daily, weekly, or monthly sales, the median is a more accurate central tendency than the average.

CALCULATING THE MODE

The third measure of central tendency is the **mode,** which is the value that appears most frequently in a distribution. As a supplemental test, the mode is helpful in deciding whether conclusions are accurate.

---

mode—the value that appears most often in a distribution.

If a list contains no values that appear more than once, there is no mode. An example is the number of transactions processed during each of six months in your department. Because no single value was repeated, there is no mode. When more than one value appears more than once, they are both modes. An example is the list of absent days per employee during the year. On that list, the values 9 and 4 each appeared twice; this is a bimodal distribution.

The mode can be used to calculate likely future events in a way similar to the median. In some cases, the median will be an inaccurate representation of what is likely to occur in the future.

Example: You are calculating the likely amount of future sales per customer. Your computerized list reports sales for the last year, arranged in ascending order. But, you notice, a large number of those sales included discounts of 10 percent. This occurred during a one-time promotional sale, which will not be repeated in the future. This factor distorts both the average and the median. The value that appears most often on the list is $35.95, which is full retail value for the product you sell most often (and most customers are expected to pay full price in the future and to buy only one item per sale). The value $35.95 is the mode for your list.

MEASURING DISPERSION

The distribution of values you use in projecting future events is a troublesome factor because the greater the degree of variance in your list, the less predictable your estimates will be. In using past values to make predictions, exceptions are often the rule.

You often need to measure the degree of variance in the values being used. **Dispersion,** also called the **spread,** is a measurement of a distribution's predictability.

----

dispersion or **spread**—the degree of difference between values in a distribution and the average.

One method for calculating dispersion is to isolate the range of values. This is done by subtracting the lowest value in the distribution from the highest value.

Example: Two departments each process varying numbers of transactions each month. However, the range for each is quite different, partly because of the different types of transactions involved:

Month	Department A	Department B
Jan	3,301	6,802
Feb	3,419	1,523
Mar	2,880	4,569
Apr	3,109	274
May	3,611	1,884
Jun	3,598	5,203
Jul	3,472	3,715
Aug	3,504	1,155

The range dispersion in each case is calculated by subtracting the smallest value from the largest value:

	Department A	Department B
Largest	3,611	6,802
Smallest	2,880	274
Dispersion	731	6,528

The problem with range dispersion is that it does not lead you to a useful solution. It does show the highest and lowest number, but cannot be used to accurately predict future transaction levels or to tell you how unpredictable your predictions are. We know that Department B has greater volatility in its transaction load than Department A. But you need to define dispersion so that the dependability of an estimate can be determined.

One way to do this is to eliminate the effects of extremely large or small numbers in a distribution by isolating values in the middle and dropping the highest and lowest values from the list. Dropping values that are exceptions to what you consider "normal" reduces the dispersion factor, making your future projections less volatile.

Applying this technique to the two lists of transactions processed in the last example, first arrange the distributions in numerical order:

	Department A	Department B
1.	3,611	6,802
2.	3,598	5,203
3.	3,504	4,569
4.	3,472	3,715
5.	3,419	1,884
6.	3,301	1,523
7.	3,109	1,155
8.	2,880	274

You will reduce the effects of widely varying values by ignoring the highest and lowest ones on the list. For example, the first, second, seventh, and eighth values can be ignored so that the range consists of only four middle values. This altered range, representing only the middle two quarters of the total list, is referred to as the *interquartile range*.

The interquartile range dispersion for each department is:

Department A:	3,504	−	3,301	=	203
Department B:	4,569	−	1,523	=	3,046

Although the degree of variance from the average is still significantly higher in Department B, it is much less than the full range spread. By eliminating the largest and smallest values, the study of range is made easier.

Although this method does away with the extremes on your list, to measure dispersion accurately you will still need to perform a calculation involving all the values. There are two ways to do this. The first method, **mean absolute deviation,** involves figuring out how far each value is from the mean (average).

----

   mean absolute deviation—a calculation that shows the average of distances between the squares of the values and the mean of a distribution.

Example: Over the past five months, the number of employees in your division has varied between 26 and 37 people. You are attempting to calculate mean absolute deviation as part of a payroll expense projection.

Month	Number
1	35
2	26
3	27
4	37
5	35

Begin by calculating the distance between each value and the mean, and then find the square of each distance. It does not matter whether the distance is positive or negative:

Month	Employees	Mean	Distance	Square
1	35	32	3	9
2	26	32	6	36
3	27	32	5	25
4	37	32	5	25
5	35	32	3	9
Total				104

Mean absolute deviation can be calculated by simply figuring out the average of the squared distances:

$$\frac{9 + 36 + 25 + 25 + 9}{5} = 20.8$$

This is the dispersion factor. Later, we see how this can be translated into the number of employees or percentage of variance.

The formula for mean absolute deviation is shown in summation notation in Figure 2-3. The subscript symbols are for the number of values on the list, and the x with a bar across the top represents the mean.

Figure 2-3. Mean absolute deviation.

$$D = \left[\frac{(v - \bar{x})_1^2 + (v - \bar{x})_2^2 + \cdots + (v - \bar{x})_n^2}{n} \right]$$

D = dispersion factor
v = value
$\bar{x}$ = mean
n = number of values

Another method used to calculate the dispersion factor is called the **variance.** This method saves time because you do not need to calculate the distance between each value and the mean.

----

variance—a method for calculating the degree of deviation in a distribution of values, in which the squares of values are added and the sum is divided by the number of values. The square root of the average is then subtracted from the result.

You start by adding the square of each value and dividing to find the average.

$$\frac{35^2 + 26^2 + 27^2 + 37^2 + 35^2}{5} = 1{,}044.8$$

Subtract the square of the mean from this total to arrive at the variance. The mean, 32, when squared equals 1,024. Therefore, the variance is:

$$1{,}044.8 - 1{,}024 = 20.8$$

This is the same total derived through mean absolute deviation. However, there were fewer steps involved. This becomes a significant savings in time when the distribution contains a large number of values. The formula for variance is shown in Figure 2-4.

Arriving at a dispersion factor does not really tell you the number of units (in this case, employees) or the percentage of variance. The 20.8 arrived at by mean absolute deviation and by variance calculation represents 20.8 employees squared. From this, you will need to calculate the actual number of employees in the total dispersion.

This is accomplished by finding the square root of the dispersion factor. The square root (a factor of a number that when multiplied by itself equals the number) of 20.8 is 4.6. Thus, you can conclude that the five-month record includes a dispersion, or spread, of 4.6 employees. This calculation is called the **standard deviation,** the formula for which

Figure 2-4. Variance.

$$D = \left(\frac{v_1^2 + v_2^2 + \ldots + v_n^2}{n} \right) - \sqrt{\overline{x}^2}$$

D = dispersion factor
v = value
$\overline{x}$ = mean
n = number of values

is shown in Figure 2-5. The lowercase Greek symbol sigma (σ) is used to represent standard deviation.

----

standard deviation—the number of units in a dispersion, calculated by finding the square root of the variance.

A variance may be stated as a percentage so that you can decide whether the degree of variance is large or small when measured against the mean. The percentage is determined by dividing the standard deviation by the mean and is called the **coefficient of variation:**

$$\frac{4.6}{32} = 14.4\%$$

----

coefficient of variation—the percentage of a variance, calculated by dividing the standard deviation by the mean.

Figure 2-5. Standard deviation.

$$\sigma = \sqrt{D}$$

σ = standard deviation
D = dispersion factor

The formula for the coefficient of variation is shown in Figure 2-6.
You can now define dispersion in the list of employees in your division with several statistical statements:

- The range of the list is 37 to 26.
- The range dispersion is 11 employees (37 − 26).
- The variance factor is 20.8.
- The list contains a dispersion of 4.6 employees.
- Dispersion in the list is 14.4 percent.

Whether you would consider a dispersion of 14.4 percent, or 4.6 employees, to be large or small depends on how much dispersion was experienced in other divisions or during other five-month periods. The relative volatility in the percentage directly affects the predictability of future projections. For example, you can conclude from this exercise that a projection of the number of future employees in the division will be 14.4 percent unpredictable. Another division may have a 25 percent dispersion, which makes their projections much less predictable.

Predictability can be clearly defined and given context with the use of statistics. When making reports moreover, you can clarify your information even more by reducing the numbers to simple charts or graphs. Chapter 3 shows how to convert numbers to visual summaries.

Figure 2-6. Coefficient of variation.

$$P = \frac{\sigma}{\bar{x}}$$

P = percentage of variance
σ = standard deviation
$\bar{x}$ = mean

WORK PROJECT

1. During the first nine months of the year, the customer service department got a varying number of complaints:

Jan	207	Jun	174
Feb	193	Jul	92
Mar	88	Aug	106
Apr	122	Sep	188
May	193		

Using this distribution, calculate:
a. Mean
b. Median
c. Mode

2. Your company keeps track of the number of sales calls each salesperson makes per month. A new salesperson reported the following number of calls for six months:

Jan	35
Feb	26
Mar	19
Apr	45
May	42
Jun	37
Total	204

With this information, calculate the dispersion factor using two methods:
a. Mean absolute deviation
b. Variance

3. From the answer derived in number 2, calculate:
a. Standard deviation
b. Coefficient of variation

3

Visual Summaries

The first step to finding something is knowing where to look.

—Robert Half

"Your report is a bit long," the manager said to the young clerk. "There must be five thousand words here. Couldn't you shorten it a bit?"

"I don't think so," the clerk answered, a confused expression on his face. "There are five graphs in the report, and you told me a picture is worth a thousand words."

Statistics is extremely valuable in your company. Many decisions are made just on the basis of the numbers that you report. But numbers by themselves are difficult to comprehend, notably so when the variety and significance of trends are complex. When you express statistics visually in a report, it helps the reader to grasp significance, comprehend an idea quickly, and relate your message more readily to the decision-making process.

Imagine the task of communicating the relative meaning of numbers, using words alone. It's not easy to explain how one conclusive figure is significant when compared with another unless you can also show it. That means the numbers have to be shown next to other, related numbers—from the past, from other divisions or departments, or from an acceptable norm.

BASIC VISUAL REPORTING RULES

Remember that the purpose of graphs is to express statistical information efficiently. Visual summaries give meaning to what would otherwise be flat and uninteresting as well as hard to understand. Your graph should be only as complex as it needs to be, which means that it should contain as *little* information as needed and should be appropriate to the type of information being reported.

Remember these rules for the preparation and reporting of statistical information in visual form:

1. *Keep it simple.* An overly complicated graph is hard to comprehend and may confuse an issue rather than clarify it. The less complex the graph, the better.

Example: You are preparing a report on your department's budget, and you want to explain some variances in graph form. Trying to combine all the variances on one graph will make it extremely complex; so you choose only the largest ones and prepare a graph for each. You report only two forms of information: actual expenses and budgeted expenses. These are shown for each of the months in your reporting period.

2. *Start by identifying time and value.* Most graphs express information by reducing a series of values (dollars, units, people, hours). These values are shown over a period of time, or in comparison to past periods or other divisions or departments. Thus, your graph should contain two distinct measurements. First is the value side, which is usually the vertical line of the graph. Second is the comparative, or horizontal, side. Here you show the time periods or comparisons between related factors.

3. *Balance the graph.* Try to keep the shape of your illustration as close as possible to a square. If your graph is six inches wide but only one inch high, it will not be as clear as one that is four inches wide and three inches high. This will require selecting a scale appropriate to the information.

Example: Your report explains expense trends over the last six months for accounts containing the greatest degree of variance. The dollar range is between $20,000 and $110,000 per month. A balanced graph should be as close as possible to a square shape. If it cannot be perfectly square, the length should be slightly greater than the height. You have six periods to report, but the range of values is much greater. Your graph should be set up so that the horizontal side is broken down into six or fewer segments. The closest breakdown involves divisions of $25,000—0, 25, 50, 75, 100, and 125. With these divisions, you will have six horizontal segments and six vertical segments.

If the desirable reporting format makes squaring difficult, you can adjust by extending one side or the other to a greater spacing of divisions. For example, you want to break down your values into ten groups, but will report changes over six months. Make the graph square by allowing more space between months than you allow between values.

4. *Keep your scaling consistent.* Once you identify the best possible scale for your graph, set it up so that each segment has equal value. That's the only way to accurately report your information. If scaling is not consistent, the visual summary of your numbers will be inaccurate.

In addition to maintaining the same paper size for each value, also be sure that your graphs start from a zero value. The relative change in values from one period to another is only apparent when this rule is followed.

Example: Your graph shows a change in one account from $65,000 to $85,000. This is best visualized on a graph starting at zero. If your graph starts at $60,000, the change will not appear to have the same degree of significance.

5. *Use the same scale for related graphs.* Whenever your report will contain a series of related graphs, use the same scaling. This helps the reader to understand how one trend is more or less meaningful than another related trend.

Example: You prepare a series of graphs showing actual and budgeted expenses for a number of accounts. By expressing each one on a graph of the same scale, you help your reader to understand the relative degree of variance and dollar amount.

THE LINE GRAPH

The most widely used illustration is the **line graph.** This is a square or rectangle showing value from top to bottom, and time from left to right.

The line graph should be used for any report involving values that change over time.

A simple line graph involves one form of information, such as sales, expenses, number of people, units produced or sold, or any other factor of value. The graph has one line for each period involved.

The line graph is also useful when comparing more than one form of related information. For example, you are working on a report summarizing sales trends in your company's field office. The raw data you gather are listed in the report:

Month	Units Sold	Goal
Jan	13,403	12,500
Feb	11,260	12,500
Mar	10,501	11,000
Apr	10,155	10,500
May	12,047	11,000
Jun	12,816	11,500
Jul	14,303	13,000
Aug	17,119	14,000
Sep	15,260	14,500
Oct	15,884	15,000
Nov	13,908	14,000
Dec	12,310	13,000

It may be entirely acceptable to report the numbers in this format and then proceed to other sections of the report, or to interpret the trend with narratives. But any interpretation will be much easier to explain if you can refer to a visual summary and not just to a listing of values. From the numerical list of units sold and goal for each month only, the real trend is difficult to spot. The line graph is an excellent tool for helping your reader to visualize the trend.

Figure 3-1 shows how easily this is achieved. The solid line represents sales, and the broken line is the goal for each month. Several points should be made concerning this graph:

1. It's simple to comprehend. A reviewer could quickly identify what it shows—actual sales versus goals over a one-year period of time.

Figure 3-1. Line graph.

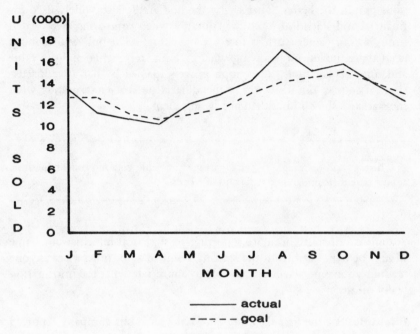

2. Value and time are specifically identified on the graph. The units sold, or value, are shown on the left vertical line, and the time periods are listed along the bottom.
3. The shape of the graph is rectangular, with the length slightly greater than the height. This is an acceptable form. Imagine the awkward appearance of this graph if units sold were broken down by one-thousand rather than by two-thousand segments. It would be twice the height.
4. The scaling is consistent. If values above 10,000 units were spaced differently from those below 10,000, information would be distorted.
5. The scaling is comfortable and comprehensible. If the report also contains related graphs for other information (such as units sold versus goals for other divisions), the same scaling should be used.

The less supplementary information someone needs to understand your graph, the better. That's why the line graph is so widely used for financial and statistical reporting, notably when comparing two related groupings of values (such as forecast and actual). The only explanations needed are the legend (showing what each line represents) and the value and time explanations. The graph is accompanied by narrative discussion, of course. But it's better to spend narrative space interpreting what the statistics show rather than just listing them.

----

line graph—a graph showing changes in value and movement in time, appropriate for comparative reporting of trends.

Scaling is critical to accurate reporting of statistical information. Value should be expressed from the starting point of zero; otherwise, anyone reading your report will not be able to appreciate what the information really means.

Example: For the first six months of last year, your company reported the following sales:

Month	Amount
Jan	$425,000
Feb	515,000
Mar	704,000
Apr	618,000
May	688,000
Jun	742,000

If you want to report this information in the form of a line graph, you may decide to start scaling from the lowest point in the range of values, or $400,000. The first example in Figure 3-2 shows how such a graph would appear. But that doesn't really show how the trend is evolving, because the scale doesn't extend down to zero. The second example is more accurate.

Figure 3-2.   Scaling.

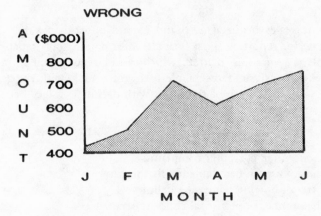

WRONG

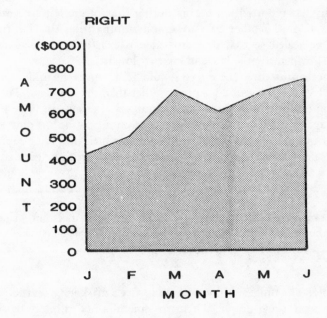

RIGHT

VARIATIONS OF LINE GRAPHS

Most value scales begin at zero and extend upward in value. That's appropriate for reporting most financial information. But statistics may also involve *negative* information, which can be reported on an inverted graph. In that case, it is acceptable to begin scaling with the zero (or starting) value at the top of the scale, with declining values beneath it. Some examples are:

- A progressive series of net losses
- The trend in customer complaints
- The amount of bad debts for six months
- A trend showing increasing debt levels
- The number of industrial accident occurrences

Another variation on the line graph places the zero value in the middle of the graph, with changes above or below. For example, your company has reported net profits during four of the last six years and net losses for the other two. A graph summarizing this information should be scaled so that the zero value is exactly in the center, with profits shown above the line and losses below it.

Another instance where zero should be shown in the middle is when your values are converted to a form other than the raw data. The most common example is to show not the numerical change in value but the percentage of change. The **percentage of change graph** is plotted by a form of indexing, a statistical technique in which one value represents 100 percent and subsequent changes are shown above or below that level.

----

percentage of change graph—a graph that summarizes information not by value but by the degree of change above or below the previous value.

Example: The units sold by your company's marketing division are to be shown on a line graph. But management is not as interested in the number of units sold as in the percentage of increase or decrease each month. Thus, the raw data for units sold must be prepared before the graph is constructed:

Month	Units Sold	Percentage Change
Jan	13,403	0%
Feb	11,260	84
Mar	10,501	93
Apr	10,155	97
May	12,047	119
Jun	12,816	106
Jul	14,303	112
Aug	17,119	120
Sep	15,260	89
Oct	15,884	104
Nov	13,908	88
Dec	12,310	89

The percentage of change is computed by dividing each month's value by the previous month's value. The first month represents 100 percent (or, on the graph, a zero value). The second month's percent change is:

$$\frac{11,260}{13,403} = 0.8401$$

Rounded to the closest one hundredth, this is 84 percent. The same computation is performed for each month. When the amount is greater than the amount for the previous month, the percentage will be greater than 100.

With the information expressed in percentage of change from one period to the next, a line graph can be used to summarize it. The first month's value (100 percent) is reported on the center line. In this form of reporting, all changes are relative to the value of the previous amount; thus, the degree of change may appear more drastic than when numbers are reported.

The test to apply before using this technique is: Does percentage of change convey information more accurately or more significantly than the actual numbers themselves? For example, the number of units sold should be reported for the purpose of judging how much sales activity changes from one month to another. If the report's intention is to judge the consistency in sales activity, percentage of change may be of more value to the reader than change in unit or dollar amounts.

Another variation on the same idea requires **indexing** the entire list of raw data. An index value of 100 is assigned to the first value, and each subsequent value is compared to it. An index of the list of units sold in the last example looks like this:

Month	Units Sold	Index Value
Jan	13,403	100
Feb	11,260	84
Mar	10,501	78
Apr	10,155	76
May	12,047	90
Jun	12,816	96
Jul	14,303	107
Aug	17,119	128
Sep	15,260	114
Oct	15,884	119
Nov	13,908	104
Dec	12,310	92

The number of units sold each month is divided by the number of units sold during the first month (the 100 index value) and multiplied by 100. This index is graphed in Figure 3-3.

----

indexing—a statistical technique in which values are reduced to percentage changes in comparison to a starting point or base value of 100.

Figure 3-3.   Indexed line graph.

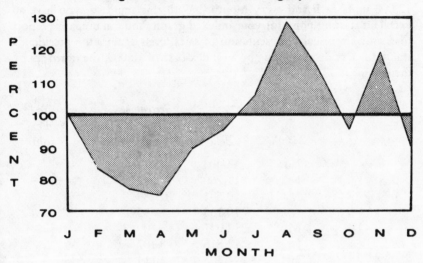

Use of an index rather than an ever-changing base each month (as in the percent change approach) will solve some of the problems you will encounter in interpreting raw data. Assigning a base of 100 to the first value adds an element of uniformity to the graph. But you continue to face a problem whenever indexing information—determination of validity for the first value. How do you know that January's volume of units sold is a fair choice for a starting point?

With most types of business data, you cannot know whether or not a single month's results can be used to accurately judge subsequent months. Be very careful in using any form of indexing; the starting point you do use must be an acceptable base for the rest of the raw data. Otherwise, the report's conclusions and the graphs you draw for them may not represent the real trend or communicate raw data in a meaningful or accurate form. This problem is overcome when a well-understood standard is applied. If you prepare an indexed graph, explain what your graph compares.

Example: You are preparing a graph for the number of units sold during the past year. The president of the company states that he wants a report showing sales in comparison to a standard he has set: "We should sell 12,000 units each and every month." With this standard, you have an excellent starting point for your indexed graph. You can prepare a report that shows a visual representation of sales levels against the president's standard. Divide each value by an index base of 12,000, the norm set by the president:

Month	Units Sold	Percentage of Standard
Jan	13,403	112%
Feb	11,260	94
Mar	10,501	88
Apr	10,155	85
May	12,047	100
Jun	12,816	107
Jul	14,303	119
Aug	17,119	143
Sep	15,260	127
Oct	15,884	132
Nov	13,908	116
Dec	12,310	103

We have looked at several different versions of the same list, each suggesting vastly different conclusions. A comparison of the line graphs you could prepare by manipulating the raw data with these different techniques would lead to very different results. This is one of the most troublesome aspects of statistical reporting. Your greatest task is identifying the most valid version of data and then deciding how to express it. If your assumptions are incorrect, or if the indexing method does not show the right trend, then your report will not be right either.

Take great care to examine your information and the results of indexing to ensure that you do not convey the wrong conclusions to management. Interpreting two differently indexed versions of the same information, you could conclude that a trend is either positive or negative. Your graph should reflect what is really occurring in the trend.

The solution is to (1) understand thoroughly the raw data you work with before interpreting them, (2) select the most appropriate type of graph and indexing method, and (3) ensure that the starting point for indexing is a valid base for the rest of the raw data.

Another problem arises when two related forms of information are reported on the same graph but require different scales. Although the simple graph is always more desirable than the complicated one, you cannot always avoid combining information.

Example: An examination of your company's manufacturing division reveals that the percentage of defects has risen during the latest month. The vice-president asks you to prepare a report studying this trend. You summarize the defects for a six-month period. During the first three months, the percentage was fairly consistent; then it dropped for two months and suddenly rose again.

Month	Units Produced	Percentage Defective
Jan	14,303	6.4%
Feb	12,417	6.2
Mar	12,109	6.7
Apr	11,551	4.3
May	10,460	5.5
Jun	15,307	8.3

Your first impulse is to prepare two separate line graphs, one for the number of units produced and one for the percentage of defective units. But then you realize that this doesn't show anything new. The vice-president already has this information. The volume and defect trends are related, however, as you discover. By preparing a single line graph showing production and defects together, you can interpret and show what the trend means.

The multiple-scale graph in Figure 3-4 shows that the rate of defects tends to change with the volume level. One possibility is that when production activity rises, workers are under greater pressure to fill orders; thus, more defective units are produced. Although your report may not state this as a definite conclusion, it does indicate a possibility worth investigating. With this information in hand, management can

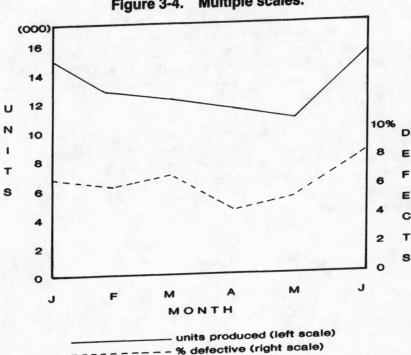

Figure 3-4. Multiple scales.

explore ways to reduce the rate of defects even when production sched-
ules are accelerated; or, the conclusion may be reached that the trend is
not negative at all.

When preparing a multiple-scale graph, remember these guidelines:

1. *Avoid more than two scales.* If you want to compare three or more
related factors or values, avoid using a line graph. Simplicity is the key
to effective visual summaries, and a two-scale graph is complicated
enough.

2. *Keep the trend lines separate.* Avoid scaling your graph in such a
way that the two trend lines cross. That will make the graph too
confusing. If necessary, extend the scale so that the two lines are well

apart, but keep the distance short enough for related movements to be plainly visible.

3. *Annotate the graph carefully*. The two top-to-bottom values should be carefully separated and explained. In Figure 3–4, the number of units are represented by a solid line, and the legend beneath the graph mentions the left scale. The broken line denotes the percentage of defects, and the right scale is mentioned in the legend.

BAR GRAPHS

The line graph is used for showing changes in value over time—by month, quarter, or year. But many forms of statistical summaries are comparisons that do not involve time movement:

- Financial information for separate divisions, subsidiaries, regions, or departments
- Reports of whole-year results for a company showing segments of sales, costs, expenses, and profit rather than month-to-month changes
- Sales for a single month comparing a number of sales offices or regions

In each of these cases, a line graph cannot be used because there is no time movement. The **bar graph** is appropriate for these types of reports.

---

bar graph—a graph used to report information that involves comparisons between related units rather than time periods.

Example: You are working on a report summarizing last year's sales. Four divisions are involved. You want to summarize actual and budgeted sales for the year for each of the four divisions. In this case, a bar graph would accomplish your goal. Results for last year were:

Division	Actual Sales	Budgeted Sales
A	$14,807,900	$13,000,000
B	12,315,400	13,500,000
C	9,558,000	10,000,000
D	4,203,000	6,000,000

These results can be summarized with two forms of bar graphs—vertical or horizontal. Either may be used to express the same information, and to a degree it is a matter of personal preference. When your statistical base is limited to two factors (such as actual and budgeted amounts), the **vertical bar graph** may be preferable because it shows values from top to bottom. This format is the same as that used in line graphs and may be more recognizable to someone looking at your report.

---

vertical bar graph—a bar graph that shows values from top to bottom and comparative data from left to right.

A vertical bar graph for this example is shown in Figure 3-5. Note that both the top-to-bottom and left-to-right lines are clearly marked for what they show and that the legend explains what the different shadings represent.

The **horizontal bar graph** may be a better choice when comparative data contain three or more elements. Placing the values from left to right and comparative segments from top to bottom may clarify information for your reader.

---

horizontal bar graph—a bar graph that shows values from left to right and comparative data from top to bottom.

Figure 3-5. Vertical bar graph.

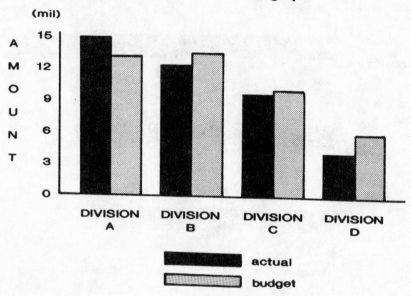

Example: The four divisions being studied in your report are compared strictly on the basis of sales. The president asks for a more expanded report showing statistics for sales, direct costs, and expenses during the most recently completed year. The graph you want to include should show these three results for each of the four divisions in such a way that they can be judged next to one another. The information for your graph is:

Division	Sales	Direct Costs	Expenses
A	$14,807,000	$8,584,600	$4,746,100
B	12,315,400	7,388,100	3,716,500
C	9,558,000	6,004,900	2,504,000
D	4,203,000	2,310,500	1,483,400

A horizontal bar graph that summarizes these raw data is shown in Figure 3-6. In this case, a more complicated grouping of information is

Figure 3-6.   Horizontal bar graph.

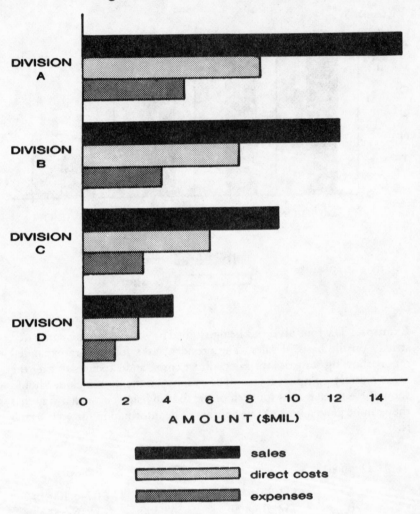

summarized concisely, with various shadings explained in the legend. This type of graph is also appropriate for comparing an even larger body of raw data.

The bar graph is easily adapted to financial status reports and statistical interpretations. It is also useful for summarizing a large body of statistical information to express the relative frequency of events.

Example: You are preparing a study for the personnel department involving the average monthly salaries for 809 full-time employees in your company. The purpose is to estimate the relative frequency of salaries within a specified range and to show the statistical information as visually as possible. Your raw data are divided into monthly salary ranges:

Monthly Range	Number of People	Total Amount
$ 0–1,000	0	$ 0
1,001–2,000	243	396,804
2,001–3,000	416	1,109,415
3,001–4,000	104	337,453
4,001–5,000	35	156,180
5,001–6,000	11	58,385
Total	809	$2,058,217

Most of us are accustomed to dealing with dollar values in reports, which is the most common form of analysis. So the most obvious graph idea would probably be to show the dollar values in some form. But when you consider the purpose of the study, you will see that the amounts by themselves provide no real meaningful information. What is of interest is the number of *people* within each salary range. Thus, the most informative type of graph would be one showing the number of employees in each salary range. For this purpose, a bar graph called a **frequency diagram** is useful.

----

frequency diagram—a variation of a bar chart that shows the number of events occurring within a specified grouping of possible ranges.

Figure 3-7.   Frequency diagram.

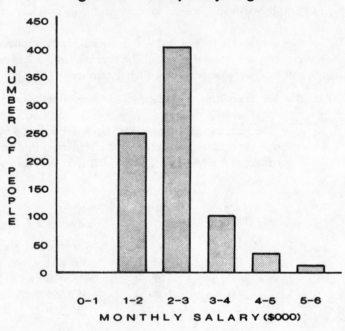

In this example, the number of "events" is the number of employees earning monthly salaries within each salary range. The graph in Figure 3-7 summarizes the data in a way that helps explain the statistical facts.

A closely related graph is the **frequency polygon,** which is a line graph of the same information as that presented in the frequency diagram, but dots replace bars at the midpoint of the range and are then connected. This shows you the shape of the statistical information.

----

frequency polygon—a graph used in place of the frequency diagram in which a trend or statistical average is plotted from one range midpoint to another, with a result similar in appearance to a line graph.

With the same information as that presented for the frequency diagram involving monthly salaries for 809 employees, you can easily prepare a frequency polygon (see Figure 3-8).

THE CIRCLE GRAPH

Besides line graphs and bar graphs, information of some types can be summarized in circular form. The **circle graph,** also popularly known as the **pie chart,** is useful when you want to present the following:

- A breakdown of where the average dollar of annual revenue is spent
- A summary of employees by education level
- Average percentage of time spent by employees in a division of tasks of routines

Figure 3-8. Frequency polygon.

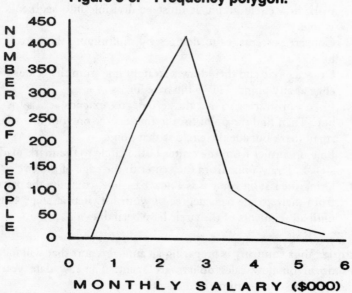

The circle graph requires more computing than other types of illustrations, as well as additional equipment. You can prepare a line graph or bar graph with a pen and a ruler; for the circle graph, you need a compass to draw the circle and a protractor to figure out the degrees. Virtually every application in which the circle graph works requires that you first reduce statistics to percentages of a whole, and then convert those percentages to the equivalent number of degrees of the circle, with the total equaling 360.

----

circle graph—a graph that shows statistical information in a circle, with divisions made for each of the segments in degrees totaling 360.

Converting information to a circle graph involves these steps:

1. Convert raw data into percentage form. For the information to work in a circle graph, it must be divisible into segments of a whole.
2. Convert percentages to degrees by multiplying the percentages by 360°.
3. Draw a circle and then draw a straight line from the center to the edge at any point. This is the base line.
4. Place a protractor so that the zero degree extends across the base line. Then find the point for the first degree on your list. Make a small mark outside the circle at that point.
5. Line up a ruler from the center of the circle to the mark made in step 4. Draw a line from the center to the edge of the circle.
6. Using the last line drawn as a new base line, compute the distance from there to the next degree on your list. Repeat steps 4 and 5 until all segments of the circle have been drawn.

Example: Your company is preparing an annual report that will include a breakdown on how sales dollars are spent. The raw data you are supplied include these summarized results:

Total sales	$14,807,900
Direct labor	3,998,200
Merchandise	4,586,400
Selling expenses	1,776,900
Operating expenses	2,969,200
Income taxes	444,300
Net profit	1,032,900

This information could simply be listed in the annual report without any explanation or elaboration. But it would be far more interesting for stockholders to be able to *see* where the money was spent. This can be achieved with a circle graph.

First, convert the financial results to percentages: Divide each number by the total sales amount, and then round to the closest whole percentage of sales that it represents:

	Amount	*Percentage*
Total sales	$14,807,900	100%
Direct labor	3,998,200	27
Merchandise	4,586,400	31
Selling expenses	1,776,900	12
Operating expenses	2,969,200	20
Income taxes	444,300	3
Net profit	1,032,900	7
Total		100%

Next, convert the percentage of each category to degrees. A circle contains 360 degrees:

	Percentage					*Degrees*
Direct labor	27%	×	360	=	97°
Merchandise	31	×	360	=	112
Selling expenses	12	×	360	=	43
Operating expenses	20	×	360	=	72
Income taxes	3	×	360	=	11
Net profit	7	×	360	=	25
Total	100%				360°

With this information, you can prepare a circle graph (see Figure 3-9).

Figure 3-9. Circle graph.

EACH DOLLAR OF SALES

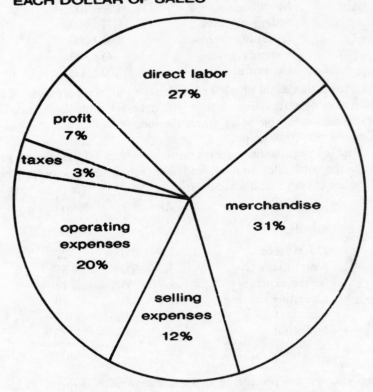

The circle graph is not appropriate in some situations. For example, you would not want to try to show a trend involving several periods; nor would you use it to compare separate divisions. A four-division sales summary divided into a circle would not be as meaningful as the same information reduced to a bar graph.

ELABORATED GRAPHS

The circle graph is more involved, and perhaps more dramatic, than other forms of graphing. It expresses information in a way that enables the reader to *see* its significance. If you will be preparing graphs without professional design help, the line, bar, and circle graphs will suffice in most situations. But when you want to dramatize or emphasize information to a greater degree, you can add a three-dimensional effect to the graphs you prepare.

A simple line graph can be made much more interesting than a flat rectangle and line by drawing a few extra lines. The resulting 3-D effect does require greater planning and execution time than the simpler, more common forms; but in some circumstances, the extra work is worth the effort, if only because it brings flat statistics to life.

Example: The growth in sales volume and profits for the first of four divisions in your company has been substantial. A section of your report dealing with the rapid and successful expansion of this division would be enhanced with a three-dimensional summary of sales, direct costs, and expenses over the last six years. Your raw data:

| | *Division A ($ Million)* | | |
Year	Sales	Costs	Expenses
1	$ 6.4	$3.7	$2.0
2	8.1	5.1	3.9
3	9.3	5.7	4.1
4	12.4	7.3	4.0
5	12.9	7.5	4.3
6	14.8	8.6	4.7

These raw data are summarized in the 3-D line graph shown in Figure 3-10.

When raw data are reported in comparative form, and not over a period of time, you can add a 3-D effect to a bar graph. For example, you want to compare last year's sales to forecast amounts for four divisions (for the same information reported on the vertical bar graph in Figure 3-5). Compare the bar graph with the one shown in Figure 3-11.

Statistical reporting can be improved, clarified, and made more interesting when information is expressed in visual form. Even if you already know that, you may be inhibited from preparing graphs to represent statistical information. The drafting skills and time required

Figure 3-10.   3-D line graph.

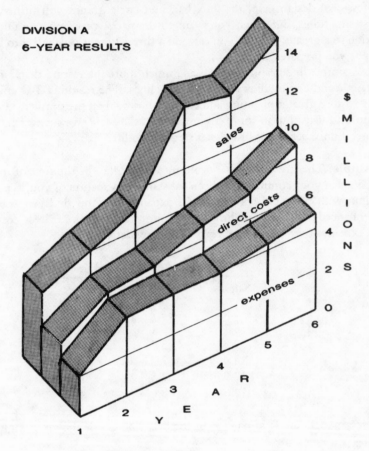

DIVISION A
6-YEAR RESULTS

often prevent managers from enhancing reports, as they should, with graphs.

Preparing a simple graph to boil down information is not a difficult task. Your graphs do not have to look like the professionally prepared color illustrations found in annual reports and published company liter-

Figure 3-11. 3-D bar graph.

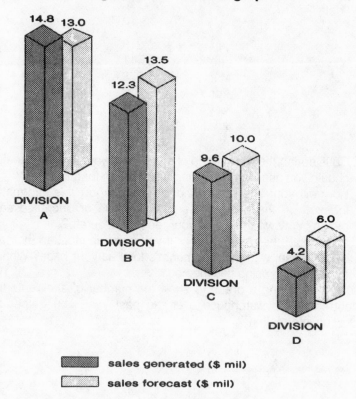

ature. You can effectively convey your message using a pen, a ruler, and a sheet of grid-ruled paper.

WORK PROJECT

1. You are asked to prepare a report summarizing the number of transactions your department processed over the last six months,

as part of a conversion from manual to automated processing. Your raw data:

Jan	6,215
Feb	9,411
Mar	4,678
Apr	3,009
May	12,615
Jun	8,451

a. Considering the wide range of numbers in your list, what scaling should you use in constructing a line graph for this report?
b. How will your line graph change if you show this information indexed on the basis of percent increase or decrease each month? Why will this make your report inaccurate?
c. How would the graph appear if you used an indexed increase or decrease, with the first month's total as your base? What is the danger in using this method?

2. You are preparing a graph to show the number of accidents that occurred in the warehouse over the past year. You gather the following information:

Jan	22	Jul	14
Feb	8	Aug	15
Mar	13	Sep	26
Apr	34	Oct	9
May	17	Nov	84
Jun	2	Dec	15

Because most of the months contain numbers below 40, your first draft of a graph includes value divisions of 5, 10, 15, 20, 25, 30, 35, 40, and 85. This makes it easy to maintain an approximately square shape.

a. What is wrong with the value scaling, and how should it be altered?
b. How can you solve the problem of maintaining an approximately square shape in your graph?

c. This graph shows a negative factor. What alternative graphing technique can be used in this case?

3. You are preparing a circle graph for a report concerning how employees spend their time. Your research leads you to the following conclusions:

Activity	Hours
Recurring routines	16.3
Meetings	3.0
Problem solving	9.4
Discussions with others	1.6
Discussions with boss	0.6
Coffee breaks	0.5
Idle time	8.6
Total	40.0

Explain the steps you need to take to convert this information to a form appropriate for a circle graph.

4
Predicting the Future

The theory of probabilities is at bottom nothing but common sense reduced to calculus.

—Pierre Simon de Laplace

"Our company's president built a financial empire on the 50-50 future theory," the manager told a new employee.

"Oh, you mean he used probability analysis to forecast and make business decisions?"

"No, nothing like that," the manager answered. "I mean he believes that every $50 raise he doesn't give you increases future profits by the same amount."

If you could predict the future with consistency and accuracy, you wouldn't have to go to the office. You could do better in Las Vegas, on Wall Street, or at the track. But because the possible outcomes of future events are random or uncertain, prediction is not a precise art.

Narrowing the odds, though, is possible. By identifying the degree of possibility connected to a future event, you can improve your business judgment. Intuition and common sense are your strongest tools; but you often face decisions that cannot be made easily because the possible outcome involves a number of variables and a lot of uncertainty. The mathematical techniques involved in probability analysis will help you improve your decision-making skills.

An important point to keep in mind: The math involved in estimating the future, no matter how scientifically executed, is a secondary skill.

Of greater importance is the premise on which you base your study. Because you must begin your analysis with a series of numbers, the risk is that your assumptions may be flawed. Thus, before applying the techniques involved, examine your assumptions and test the information you use.

Explanations of probability usually start out with the analogy to a coin toss. If you toss a coin once, you have a 50-50 chance that heads will come up. If you toss the coin 100 times, the *average* outcome will be 50 heads and 50 tails. But it's not certain that you will have that exact result; it's only the average.

The coin toss is a popular example in explanations of statistics because it is based on a very important assumption: that the test is fair. If you examine the coin to make sure that one side is heads and the other is tails, then you have every reason to believe there's a 50-50 chance of either side coming up.

In a business application, things are not as simple. For example, you want to determine the probability that sales volume will be greater or less than previous years' averages. As long as the average is fair (conditions are roughly the same for each year), there is a 50-50 chance of either event taking place. But it's likely that conditions today are not the same as in the past, so a 50-50 test would not apply.

The coin toss example makes the point about the theory of probability, but it doesn't show you how to apply the theory in a business decision. You already know that few of the problems you must solve are so clear that only one of two results will occur. You face too many variables.

You can use probability analysis for even the most complex decisions. Here we start out with a 50-50 example, but only to introduce the more advanced applications of probability for the same problem. Remember these points as you proceed:

1. *Probability involves many intangibles.* In a business situation, few problems involve only the surface argument. Many subtle considerations may enter the equation.

   Example: A construction firm plans to bid on an estimated 18 projects during the coming year. On the basis of previous years' averages, 9 projects will be won. This estimate can be expressed as a 50-50 chance of winning each contract. But you also need to consider a number of other possibilities, such as:

- Competition will be stronger in the future than in the past.
- Fewer than 18 projects will be available during the coming year.
- Some competitors will have an inside advantage on certain jobs.
- Economic conditions will be better or worse than in the past.

2. *Probability is only one of many tools.* Your intuition, common sense, and business experience will affect every decision you make. Probability analysis is helpful in narrowing down the likely outcomes in the future, but it is not the last word.
3. *There are no guarantees.* Even when the odds favor one outcome to an extreme, there is no certainty that the outcome will follow the averages. Opportunity and risk are constant companions in business. You can beat the averages and excel; or you can lose because of a string of bad luck.

THE 50-50 CHANCE

If business decisions could be expressed in absolute terms, without the intangible considerations or the outside influences we have to remember, there could be only two outcomes. An event would occur, or it would not.

The study of **probability** involves the likelihood of a range of possible outcomes among all possible events. Some isolated outcomes can be defined in extremes (they will never occur, or they will always occur). But in between these two, a number of other possibilities exist. For example, a food manufacturer will develop a number of products in the future; some will be profitable, others will not. It's certain that products will be developed and test-marketed. It's certain that the company will never market a product without first testing it. But the degree of profit or loss will never be certain. Every product will vary in performance.

---

probability—the likelihood of one or more outcomes among the possible range of events that could occur.

Identifying the possible outcomes in any decision is essential to realistic probability analysis. It's rare for a range to be limited to just two outcomes; in many situations, there could be a very large number of results. The number of units sold in a year could extend from zero to infinity; the possible range of outcomes is huge. That range is narrowed by eliminating the outside extremes and then classifying the limited remainder into groups of a specified size, such as 1,000 units.

---

outcome—an event within a range of possible events, the probability of which is judged in comparison to the entire range.

Example: Your company is thinking about offering a new product line and wants you to attend a meeting to discuss the idea. The big question, of course, is whether or not adding a specific product is likely to be a profitable decision. So on a very preliminary level, the problem can be expressed in simplified, but absolute, terms. There are two possible outcomes:

1. The new product line will be profitable.
2. The new product line will not be profitable.

You could limit your study to the probability of success or failure. On the surface, that's a 50-50 possibility, at least without exploring the related facts. There are only two outcomes. In truth, the likelihood of profitability is tied to competitive factors, costs of production and marketing, consumer acceptance or rejection, and a wide range of other influencing factors.

When those factors are taken into account, you may have better than a 50-50 chance of success, or worse than a 50-50 chance. To demonstrate how probability analysis works, however, let's assume that success and failure both have an equal chance. This is the same probability as a coin toss. It may come up either heads or tails, just as a new product line may either succeed or fail.

This oversimplified example demonstrates a very important business principle: A BUSINESS SUCCEEDS BY SELECTING THE MOST PROMISING TASKS. If all risks were 50-50, then you would expect that, on average, projects would succeed half the time and fail the other half. If that happened consistently, companies would always break even on average because profits and losses would offset one another. But if you analyze risks and then pursue those with odds better than 50-50, you will have more successes than failures.

THE LIKELY OUTCOME

Better-than-average risks can be identified by dividing likely outcomes into a number of groups and then analyzing them mathematically. The most likely outcomes should be placed in the middle range, with outcomes less likely below and above.

Example: You work for a food manufacturing sales company that has developed and marketed more than 800 products over the last 20 years. Of these, only about 120 have failed. On average, 85 percent of all new products have been profitable. As long as management selects new product lines using the same criteria as in the past, and as long as prevailing conditions have not changed, it's fair to assume that there's an 85 percent chance of success, or an 85-15 probability.

You may not know exactly how those past marketing decisions were made, and the marketing environment may have changed as well. For example, if a major competitor is taking a rapidly growing market share, perhaps it's not realistic to expect that 85 percent success record to continue.

Business decisions involve much more than simply the issue of profit and loss, even though that's the central question and concern. The decision whether or not to market a new product is made from an evaluation of risk. And that's where probability analysis is most useful.

Rather than investing a huge amount of money to introduce new products nationally, your company tests the market in isolated regions to judge future profitability. This technique is given many names, but it's a form of probability analysis. A product may be tested by investing a relatively small amount of capital in a sample market. The results indicate whether or not a larger investment is justified. This is an example of making a decision on the basis of better than 50-50 odds.

Probability based on one of two outcomes can be thought of as the first level of analysis. A product will be profitable, or it will not. If the range of possible outcomes is expanded (for example, very profitable or very unprofitable), a second level comes into the picture, and analysis is then performed with that higher number of outcomes in mind.

Example: During a meeting to discuss a new product line, you accept the assignment to perform a probability study in the test markets. Based on a scaled-down version of a national marketing campaign, the break-even point for the test markets is identified as 1,001 units sold during one week. If that level is exceeded, then the consensus is that the product will be profitable. Most products have historically sold between 1,001 and 2,500 units during one-week market tests. But you are aware of probabilities both above and below those levels; so you break down the likely outcome into nine groups, with the most likely outcomes in the middle:

1. No sales volume
2. Sales volume from 1 to 500 units
3. Sales volume from 501 to 1,000 units
4. Sales volume from 1,001 to 1,500 units
5. Sales volume from 1,501 to 2,000 units
6. Sales volume from 2,001 to 2,500 units
7. Sales volume from 2,501 to 3,000 units
8. Sales volume from 3,001 to 3,500 units
9. Sales volume above 3,500 units

The first and last outcomes have never occurred in the past. However, you recognize that any of the possible outcomes *could* happen and have a chance of taking place in either of the two test markets.

Most products historically have sold between 1,001 and 2,500 units per test week. Thus, you know that outcomes 4, 5, and 6 are the most likely outcomes. As the outcomes move away from this middle ground, likelihood declines:

Least likely	1
Less likely	2 and 3
Most likely	4, 5, and 6
Less likely	7 and 8
Least likely	9

We previously said that all nine outcomes have a chance of occurring. That's not the same as what is *likely* to occur. There is an important distinction that's best demonstrated by studying the possible combinations mathematically. Use the numerical name of each outcome category as its mathematical value: Outcome number 1 is given a mathematical value of 1; outcome number 9 is given a value of 9.

Because there are two test markets and they cannot be expected to act in exactly the same manner, the possible outcomes should be defined as they might occur in both markets collectively. There are 45 possible combinations of outcomes, distinguished by the assigned numerical value for each of the nine possible outcomes. They are:

1 and 1	2 and 8	5 and 5
1 and 2	2 and 9	5 and 6
1 and 3	3 and 3	5 and 7
1 and 4	3 and 4	5 and 8
1 and 5	3 and 5	5 and 9
1 and 6	3 and 6	6 and 6
1 and 7	3 and 7	6 and 7
1 and 8	3 and 8	6 and 8
1 and 9	3 and 9	6 and 9
2 and 2	4 and 4	7 and 7
2 and 3	4 and 5	7 and 8
2 and 4	4 and 6	7 and 9
2 and 5	4 and 7	8 and 8
2 and 6	4 and 8	8 and 9
2 and 7	4 and 9	9 and 9

It doesn't matter whether one side of an outcome occurs in the first region or the second. The purpose of this exercise is to define probability. Thus, if 3,500 units sell in the first test market region and 1,500 in the second, the result is the same as if the volume for each region were reversed.

To examine the probability and assess risk (calculating the outcome), you will need to express the range of outcomes mathematically. You have assigned numerical value to the nine groups, with the most likely outcome in the center. Those below that level represent less likely and less profitable outcomes; and those above are less likely but more profitable ones. There is a very slim probability that both test markets will have a 1 outcome, resulting in a combined outcome with a numerical value of 2—meaning that in both markets, no units were sold during the first week. But that *is* one possible outcome.

Historical sales levels indicate that it's just as unlikely that both test markets will have a 9 outcome, the combined result of which would be the highest numerical value, 18. That would mean that both test markets exceeded past records. Again, it's still one of the possibilities, so it is included in the study.

The next step is to arrange the possible outcomes in order of total combined numerical value:

Outcome	Value	Outcome	Value
1 and 1	2	4 and 6	10
1 and 2	3	5 and 5	10
1 and 3	4	2 and 9	11
2 and 2	4	3 and 8	11
1 and 4	5	4 and 7	11
2 and 3	5	5 and 6	11
1 and 5	6	3 and 9	12
2 and 4	6	4 and 8	12
3 and 3	6	5 and 7	12
1 and 6	7	6 and 6	12
2 and 5	7	4 and 9	13
3 and 4	7	5 and 8	13
1 and 7	8	6 and 7	13
2 and 6	8	5 and 9	14

Outcome	Value	Outcome	Value
3 and 5	8	6 and 8	14
4 and 4	8	7 and 7	14
1 and 8	9	6 and 9	15
2 and 7	9	7 and 8	15
3 and 6	9	7 and 9	16
4 and 5	9	8 and 8	16
1 and 9	10	8 and 9	17
2 and 8	10	9 and 9	18
3 and 7	10		

This grouping of possible outcomes for the combined two regions is called a **set**. Some sets are very small; others may be quite large. So it's important to define a set for a probability study. For example, a set with millions of parts would be treated much differently than one with only a few. You would need to use sample information rather than work with every possible outcome.

In your probability study for the new product line, the set has a range of 45 possible outcomes, which is called the **probability space** or **sample space**. The probability space is small enough that the entire set can be used in the study.

----

   set—a listing of all possible outcomes of an event.
   probability space or **sample space**—the range of possible outcomes in a set.

The set developed for possible outcomes of sales in two test markets can be presented visually on a frequency polygon as shown in Figure 4–1. Dots were placed on the polygon according to total numerical value. Because there are two regions, the combined total must be cut in half to represent the grouping in which it belongs. For example, a combined numerical value for both test markets of 16 is the equivalent of group 8; and a combined numerical value of 9 represents an outcome between groups 4 and 5.

Figure 4-1. Frequency of outcomes.

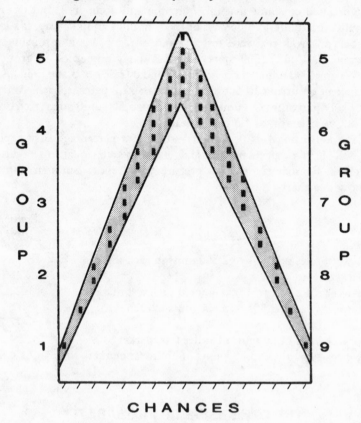

This exercise helps visualize the probabilities. The most likely outcome will be close to the middle of the range. You can identify the degree of probability by isolating and reporting the results on a percentage basis. The question to answer here is, "What is the likelihood that the product will be profitable?"

In the "most likely" range, each market is likely to sell between

1,001 and 2,500 units. By counting the number of dots on the frequency polygon, you conclude that this outcome will occur in 21 out of every 45 events, or about 46.6 percent of the time. Put another way, if a large number of products were tested, 46.6 percent would probably sell between 1,001 and 2,500 units. The less likely outcomes, in groups 2 and 3 (1 to 1,000 units) and in groups 7 and 8 (2,501 to 3,500 units), have a chance of occurring 10 out of 45 times, or 22.2 percent, each. And the least likely outcomes (no units or more than 3,500 units) may each occur in 2 out of 45 times, or 4.5 percent each.

By converting this probability study to a percentage-basis report, you will help other managers and executives to equate the odds of success in familiar terms. You prepare your report, summarizing the study with a chart:

Possible Outcome	Probability (%)
First-week sales of 1,001 to 2,500 units in each test market	46.6%
First-week sales of 1 to 1,000 units in each test market	22.2
First-week sales of 2,501 to 3,500 units in each test market	22.2
First-week sales of no units in either test market	4.5
First-week sales above 3,500 units in both test markets	4.5

THE OTHER SIDE OF PROBABILITY

Probability analysis can tell you the chances of an event taking place. Another way to look at the question is, "What are the chances of an event *not* occurring?" At the beginning of the market test example, we stated that the breakeven point was estimated at 1,001 units sold. So, based on the conclusions you reached, what is the probability that the product will not produce a profit?

The results show that there's a 22.2 percent chance of selling between 1 and 1,000 units, and a 4.5 percent chance of selling no units—as unlikely an outcome as that is. So you can conclude that given the entire spectrum of possible outcomes, there is a 26.7 percent chance—about one in four—that the new product will not be profitable.

The likelihood of an event occurring or not occurring can be narrowed even further. For example, you can revise your report by eliminating the most remote possibilities—selling no units in either region during the test week, or selling more than 3,500 units in both regions. You know these extremes are probably not going to occur. By reducing your set, you eliminate four outcomes, bringing the number of possible outcomes down from 45 to 41, and the study's conclusion can be revised on that basis. Now, instead of allowing for every possible result, your probability study is based on the most likely outcomes the product test will produce. Your revised study reads:

Possible Outcome	Probability (%)
First-week sales of 1,001 to 2,500 units in each test market	51.2%
First-week sales of 1 to 1,000 units in each test market	24.4
First-week sales of 2,501 to 3,500 units in each test market	24.4

Now the conclusion is clarified. You can evaluate the product's chances in one of three ways. The most likely outcome—sales at a profitable level and within a range conforming to past experience—has a 51.2 percent chance of occurring (21 out of 41 times). The probability that the outcome will be below that range is equal to the probability that it will be above it. You can also report that the chances of *not* making a profit are only 24.4 percent (10 out of 41). Now, with a more detailed study, the central question of risk can be addressed. There is a 75.6 percent chance that the product will be profitable—much better than 50–50.

MODIFYING THE CONCLUSION

The study to this point has been very symmetrical. The most likely outcome was placed in the middle, and outcomes above and below were mathematically balanced. With the techniques demonstrated to this point, you can weigh the groups so that your probability analysis reflects a more realistic market condition.

Example: During your meeting, the decision to test-market the new product in two regions is discussed at length. You decide that the following adjustments should be taken into account:

- Historical averages were greater several years ago, and more recent new product volumes have been lower than the average. The probability of meeting historical averages is lower today.
- There are more competitors in the same business today, and they operate in the same markets. This may further reduce the chances that past averages will be met.
- Profit margins may be lower than expected as the result of recent expansion. More units will have to be sold to reach breakeven. The estimate is that it will be necessary to sell 1,501 or more units, rather than 1,001.

With these points in mind, you can still use the nine groups used in your probability study. Rather than considering groups 4, 5, and 6 as the "middle" ranges, however, you shift the new average to groups 5, 6, and 7 to allow for the recent changes in market conditions. This is estimated to offset the adverse conditions that have developed.

Eliminating the most remote possibilities—no sales in either region and sales exceeding all past records—will alter your revised conclusion. The most likely probability, the middle group, must be increased to a range between 1,501 and 3,000 units due to an estimate of changes resulting from competition factors. The loss range is made larger, between 1 and 1,500 units. And the higher-than-average range is reduced to between 3,001 and 3,500. Instead of groups of equal size, the altered arrangement is:

Lower than average	Groups 2, 3, and 4
Profitable average	Groups 5, 6, and 7
Higher than average	Group 8

The purpose in shifting is to alter the reported probability as an attempt to take into account the way that recent changes affect outcome. Groups

1 and 9 are eliminated as the most remote outcomes, just as they were in the previous example. Now, the concluding section of your report must be adjusted for the new spread and acceptable averages. This will reduce estimates of profitability, thus changing the risk factor for the new product. Now, out of 41 possible outcomes, 21 (51.2 percent) will fall within groups 5, 6, and 7; another 18 (43.9 percent) will fall within groups 2, 3, or 4; and 2 (4.9 percent) will fall within group 8:

Possible outcome	Probability (%)
First-week sales of 1,501 to 3,000 units in each test market	51.2%
First-week sales of 1 to 1,500 units in each test market	43.9
First-week sales of 3,001 to 3,500 units in each test market	4.9

The most likely range remains at the same percentage as in the previous conclusion. But the chances that the product will be unprofitable have increased to 43.9 percent. Now, combining the two profitable groups—the first and third—the chances for profit are 56.1 percent, still better than 50–50, but perhaps more reflective of current market conditions.

The mathematical techniques needed for probability analysis are sometimes more complex than the examples given here. But for even the most complicated probability study, the real complexity is not in the formula or in the technique; it's in determining whether or not your assumptions are correct to begin with.

In the previous example, you divided likely sales volume ranges into nine groups. The hypothesis used included a series of assumptions concerning the breakeven point, average range of units, and competitive factors. This series of beliefs is referred to as the **null hypothesis.** If you question these beliefs, you need to develop an **alternative hypothesis.**

----

null hypothesis—a belief or series of beliefs used to conduct a probability study.

alternative hypothesis—a belief or series of beliefs used in place of the null hypothesis.

How do you know your beliefs are correct? You may conduct your probability study with nine divisions of possible outcomes in the belief that you fully understand breakeven, competitive factors, market demand, and what might be expected as a "normal" average for your company. Before proceeding, however, you should test your null hypothesis, using the following:

1. *Historical information.* In the preceding example, we based the first probability study on an assumption that historical averages were accurate. But the trend during recent years has been for those averages to decline. So, in order for your study to be realistic, expectations should reflect that trend.

2. *Validation.* Today's conditions may make historical averages unsuitable for use in a probability study. If competitive forces are stronger now than on average, the hypothesis should be adjusted to reflect that change. If demand factors have changed, you will also need to determine how that will affect your study. The greater the degree of influence that conditions have on the averages, the more radically your hypothesis should be changed.

3. *Modification.* The hardest part of probability analysis is deciding how to change the hypothesis. The need for modification may be obvious; but knowing to what degree a change should be made is more subjective. Averages work for analysis of unchanging conditions; but in business, conditions are changing constantly. In our example, we simply shifted the middle so that chances of a loss increased and chances of a higher-than-average profit decreased. That may be an arbitrary method, and a more methodical approach might be preferable.

Example: You began your probability study using information from past product tests and market experience. But you are also aware that volume and profits have been declining in recent years.

The way to validate your null hypothesis, or to identify a reasonable alternative hypothesis, is through testing. It would require a lot of work to plot each and every product for the last few years in terms of profit margin, sales volume, and varying demand. So instead, you take a sample and attempt to identify a trend. You pick a few products believed to represent overall volume trends and estimate today's likely conditions.

The same approach can be used to modify your hypothesis for competitive factors. By comparing market share in terms of sales volume for your company and other companies in the same industry, you can spot changing conditions over a period of years and plot the next step in the trend.

This procedure may sound like a good deal of work, and it will be if hypothesis testing is conducted on too broad a set of information. But by identifying representative sets (major competitors, typical products, and average breakeven levels), the task can be reduced to a more manageable level.

Statistics reduces the guesswork, but cannot give you a specific, absolute future outcome. More emphasis should be placed on the dependability of the hypothesis than on the manipulation of numbers, because that's where the greatest uncertainty lies.

WORK PROJECT

1. The vice-president of sales has asked for your help in developing estimates of the number of salespeople who will need to be recruited during the coming year. Three new regions are involved in the expansion plan. In the eight existing regions, estimates are always based on the previous year's figures. You begin your study by gathering first-year recruitment statistics for other regions:

Region	Salespeople Recruited During First Year
1	115
2	93
3	101
4	106
5	99
6	111
7	82
8	110

You define the range of possible outcomes as greater than 69 and less than 120, given what has occurred in other regions. This range is broken out into the following groups:

1. 70 to 79 people
2. 80 to 89 people
3. 90 to 99 people
4. 100 to 109 people
5. 110 to 119 people

You are aware that a number of combined outcomes may occur in the three new regions. For the purposes of estimating, you are not concerned with the arrangement of those outcomes. With that in mind, how many possible outcomes are there?
2. Using the information developed for the first question, divide your list of possible outcomes into a mathematical breakdown in sequence, from the lowest combination to the highest.
3. Again using the same information:
   a. Summarize the chances that each of the five outcomes will occur, in percentage form.
   b. Eliminate the first and fifth outcomes from your analysis and express the chances of each of the remaining three outcomes in percentage form.

5

Experimenting With the Uncertain

Problems increase in geometric ratio, solutions in arithmetic ratio.

—Charles Issawi

"We can never be absolutely certain about anything," Jill said to Marty. "There are always shades of gray between the black and white."

Marty thought a moment and said, "For example, if a tree falls in the forest and no one is there to hear it, does it make a sound? Is that what you mean?"

"Not exactly," Jill replied. "I mean, if a tree falls in the forest, do we have the budget to convert it to lumber, find a buyer, and get our price, all before the competition hears it hit the ground?"

You spent many days getting your information together, making sure that historical results were right and testing your hypothesis. But when the actual results came through, you found that your estimate was way off base—because the future didn't follow the trend set in the past.

Because so many aspects of the future will vary from the past, you cannot always depend on trends developed historically, even over a very long period of time. Those trends only indicate what may happen. So you have a problem with any type of forecasting: Actual results cannot

be promised or created statistically. The most you can hope for is a
scientific best guess.

A lot of errors in forecasting come from building an estimate with
flawed raw data. A sample, you will recall, must fairly represent the
population under study. If that isn't the case, then the estimate won't be
scientific, and your guess won't be the best one.

In Chapter 4, an expanded example of forecasting probabilities
demonstrated how raw data can be used to estimate the future. Possible
outcomes were divided into a number of groups and mathematically
broken down. But what if the historical averages were wrong? What if
competitive and demand factors have changed the whole picture? And
even if those changes were allowed for, what if the whole picture changes
again next month?

Whenever you develop a statistically based report dealing with
forecasts of future events, be aware of the lack of certainty that will
invariably be involved. Include with your report an explanation of the
variance that management should expect, even with the best estimate.

DEFINING VARIANCE

Most forecasting and budgeting is performed using the most basic
statistical techniques. For example, a manager attempts to predict the
coming year's budget for office supplies by reviewing the past year. If
the amount spent inches upward a bit each month, the budget continues
the apparent trend. Or the total for the year is added up and the total is
divided by 12, so that the budget represents the mean (average) of the
past year.

A prediction about future events can be better defined for management if the degree of deviation from the average is also given. To find the
degree of deviation, follow this procedure:

1. Add the squares of each value and find the average.
2. Subtract the square of the mean from the total in step 1.
3. Find the square root of the answer in step 2.
4. Divide the answer in step 3 by the mean to determine the
   percentage (coefficient of variance).

Example: The nine outcome groups defined in Chapter 4 were based on historical averages of first-week sales for ten different products selected according to the number of years on the market:

Years on Market	Units Sold First Week
20	2,672
18	1,915
16	2,006
14	2,595
12	1,811
10	1,684
8	1,619
6	1,586
4	1,474
2	1,586
Total	18,948
Mean	1,894.8

The entire probability study and definition of likely breakeven, profit, and "acceptable" results were based on the use of an average—but you don't yet know how much variation there is in that average. In other words, you must ask, "How dependable are the raw data being used? How do they compare with other raw data?"

To define the degree of variation in the raw data being used, follow these four steps:

1. Add and average the squares:

$$\frac{2{,}672^2 + 1{,}915^2 + 2{,}006^2 + 2{,}595^2 + 1{,}811^2 + 1{,}684^2 + 1{,}619^2 + 1{,}586^2 + 1{,}474^2 + 1{,}586^2}{10} = 3{,}750{,}507.6$$

2. Subtract the square of the mean:

Average of the squares	3,750,507.6
Less 1,894.8²	3,590,267.0
Difference	160,240.6

3. Find the square root of the difference: Square root of 160,240.6
   = 400.3
4. Divide the square root by the mean:

$$\frac{400.3}{1,894.8} = 21.1\%$$

You now know that the coefficient of variance is 21.1 percent. That tells you the relative degree, or volatility, of variation in the raw data. From this information, you can confidently report to management the following:

- Historical averages may vary up or down by a count of 400 units sold.
- The variance in units sold is 21.1 percent.

The degree of variation might be considered relatively stable or relatively unstable. It's all a matter of comparison. For example, if you selected a different list of products and studied their first-week sales volume, you might discover a variance of 48 percent, making the resulting report far more uncertain than the one in this example, which has less than half its degree of variance.

RANDOM EVENTS

You can convey relative degrees of dependability in a report, and you can explain the probability of one or more outcomes. But both these estimates are based on the premise that historical raw data will continue to be valid. And that is not always the case.

Some predictions cannot be grounded in the past at all. They are **random events.** The only way to judge a random event is to perform tests of outcomes as they develop. In other words, historical facts don't matter because they won't affect the future.

---

random event—an event for which all possible outcomes have equal chances of occurring.

Example: Tossing a coin any number of times, you have a 50-50 chance of a heads outcome or a tails outcome. However, each test is independent of tests performed before and after. Although it's unlikely that you will toss heads ten out of ten times, each toss is a random event, and each has a 50-50 chance of being heads or tails.

The outcome of a random event can be predicted with a number of methods. For example:

1. Choose one result for every test. You will be right 50 percent of the time, on average.
2. Choose heads for the first half of your tests and tails for the second half. Again, you will be right 50 percent of the time, on average.
3. Select a pattern, such as heads and tails in alternating tests, or groups of two, three, four, or more. You will still be right half the time and wrong half the time, on average.

An important rule concerning random events is: As long as the method of prediction represents the entire range of outcomes, the method used will not affect the outcome.

Example: You have identified six possible outcomes for the number of units that will be sold during a one-week new product test. In your opinion, each of the six outcomes has an equal chance of occurring. As long as each of the six is predicted the same number of times, you will be right, on average, one-sixth of the time and wrong five-sixths of the time.

You may conclude that there is no point in trying to predict the outcome of a random event. But remember that most of the predictions you make will have more than two possible results. Thus, it is possible to predict the most likely results by testing with a **random sample**.

----

   random sample—a sample that allows each possible outcome an equal chance of occurring.

When dealing with a large number of possible outcomes, you can isolate the most likely probabilities by making an observation: A SERIES OF RANDOM VARIABLES WILL BE INCREASINGLY MORE LIKELY TO HAVE OUT-COMES NEAR THE MIDDLE OF THE DISTRIBUTION THAN AT THE EXTREME ENDS. We saw an example of this in Chapter 4. There was a greater probability that units sold in two regions would approximate the middle range than the extreme ranges.

Another example is when two dice are rolled. There are a total of 21 possible outcomes (assuming it doesn't matter which dice comes up; for example, a 2-3 or a 3-2 outcome counts the same):

1-1	2-3	3-6
1-2	2-4	4-4
1-3	2-5	4-5
1-4	2-6	4-6
1-5	3-3	5-5
1-6	3-4	5-6
2-2	3-5	6-6

The range of possible outcomes extends from a total of 2 up to a total of 12. But the chances of those extremes coming up are limited:

Total of 2 = 1 chance, a roll of 1 and 1
Total of 12 = 1 chance, a roll of 6 and 6

In comparison, the chances of 6 or 7, the outcomes exactly in the middle, are much greater:

Total of 6 = 3 chances, rolls of:
    1 and 5
    2 and 4
    3 and 3

Total of 7 = 3 chances, rolls of:
    1 and 6
    2 and 5
    3 and 4

The same condition was found in an analysis of the nine possible outcomes in two regions (Chapter 4). The outcomes in the middle of the distribution had a greater likelihood of occurring than the extremes. It is more likely that units sold will be nearer the historical average than the extremes—no units sold or record-breaking numbers of units sold.

INDEPENDENT EVENTS

No analysis based on past events will be of value if the future event doesn't vary in accordance with the past. You depend on your ability to anticipate events before they happen. But some of the problems you face will involve **independent events.**

----

independent event—an event for which the outcome cannot be predicted on the basis of an unrelated event.

In such an instance, information developed as part of the study may not be valid in determining final results. A typical example of this is attempting to judge the outcome of a budget on the basis of three months of actual results close to estimated amounts—but not anticipating what is about to happen. Seasonal changes, unforeseen expenses, and growth in the employee base, to name a few of the possibilities, could distort what at first appears to be a dependable trend.

Example: Your product test is conducted in two regions but in different weeks. Results for the first week are much greater than the averages you expected. What does that mean in terms of how the second area's test will come out?

There are a number of possibilities. But you have no way of knowing the degree of significance, if any, of a single test of the new product. The information that sales were much higher than you expected could mean any of several things:

1. There is no special significance. Response in one area is only one of two tests. Results can be validated only by comparing them to results in the second test market.

2. Response will be better than you expected everywhere—in other test markets and nationally as well. An exceptional outcome could be a sign that market response will be positive everywhere and that the second region's results will, in fact, also exceed previous records.

3. The testing selected for this product was not adequate to judge market response. If results from the second area are vastly different from the first, that tells you that you have not yet tested enough. It may be necessary to test the product in four or five areas, or more.

Using averages for a small base of testing can be deceptive. If one region has results 20 percent higher than expected, and another 20 percent lower, then the product has performed at expected levels, but only on average. One or both markets could be unrepresentative of the market's overall response.

The same arguments can be made when results for the first test are below average. That does not necessarily indicate how a subsequent test will end up. To deal with the problems encountered when random events affect test results, follow these steps:

1. *Test adequately.* Whether developing basic raw data for your probability analysis or trying to anticipate results for a subsequent test,

first be sure that you have enough information to identify the right trend. Avoid the common mistake of jumping to a conclusion with insufficient data.

2. *Be aware of emerging changes.* If you develop averages or norms on the basis of historical information, evaluate that information with changing conditions in mind. Don't expect to make the average if influencing factors have changed the rules.

3. *Constantly modify test assumptions.* Statistical analysis is an everchanging skill. It isn't enough to develop one series of assumptions that you then apply to every case. Update each test with newly discovered information from previous tests and actual results.

LARGE AND SMALL AVERAGES

Whether testing probability of coin tosses, dice rolls, or units sold, the outcome is based on averaging. If you test the number of units sold for 10 regions instead of 2, the chances that overall results will resemble actual market responses will increase. As the field of testing is increased, the results—even of a random event—become more predictable. This statistical theory is called the **law of large numbers.** The larger your test base, the more likely it is that the mean of the outcome will be close to the mean of the random variable.

----

law of large numbers—a theory stating that when random variables are tested many times, the average outcome will fall close to the average of the random variable.

Example: An actuary sets life insurance premium rates for each age on the basis of historical studies of mortality. The exact timing of a death for any one policyholder cannot be known; but the insurance company can accurately predict how many deaths will occur each year for each age.

Each and every measurement of a random variable is independent. But a series of tests can very accurately tell when an event is likely to occur. It would be very difficult to predict deaths if only ten histories were used as the basis for the study. But when millions are used, the results of random variables can be more specifically pinned down.

We know, for example, that the average of any two numbers is computed by adding them together and dividing the sum by 2. And for one million numbers, the total must be divided by one million. The formula for average, or mean, is recalled in Figure 5-1.

You can depend on the average of a larger base to a greater degree than the average of a very small base. Unless your random variables are weighted in some manner, the outcome will have what is called a **normal distribution**. This distribution is seen in the example in Chapter 4. The frequency polygon (Figure 4-1) curves upward into the middle and then falls away.

---

normal distribution—the outcome of a probability test that produces a symmetrical result.

Figure 5-1. Average.

$$\bar{x} = \frac{x_1 + x_2 + \cdots + x_n}{n}$$

$\bar{x}$ = average
x = value
n = number of values

The typical normal distribution of probability is illustrated in Figure 5-2.

You have seen examples of a normal distribution in dice rolls and variations of the two-region product test. In each case, the curve has a normal distribution. The possible outcomes or values are identically spaced. These examples follow the rule expressed in the **central limit theorem,** a statistical concept you can use to convert probabilities into fairly isolated odds (like a better than 50-50 chance of success). We saw an example of this in the last chapter, where outcome was shown to have a greater chance of occurring in the middle of a range.

----

central limit theorem—a rule stating that the average of a set of identically spaced outcomes or values will exhibit a normal distribution.

Figure 5-2. Normal distribution.

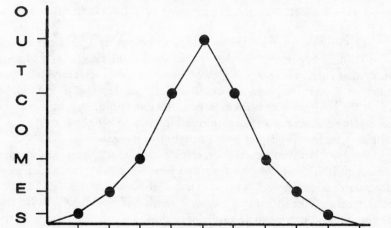

A SHORTCUT METHOD

Understanding how the law of large numbers works, you may conclude that it is always desirable to use a larger sample for a study. Although that is true, it isn't always practical to investigate an entire history.

Example: Your company has marketed about 800 products over the last 20 years. A probability analysis based on all 800 products would be time-consuming and exhausting. The solution is to limit the sample used but take three additional steps:

1. Test the hypothesis before beginning your probability study to ensure that your conclusions are right. Is it accurate to depend on past averages? Or are current conditions different enough that the information from the past should be modified?

2. Broaden the possible outcomes so that the generalities are reduced and your conclusion is more specific. Estimate likely results for two tests, but premise your study on what would occur if the product were tested in four markets. Also, break down possible outcomes into a larger number of groups.

3. Use a shortcut method to derive the most important conclusion.

The first step, testing the hypothesis, is essential if your conclusion is to contain any merit. In the case of the product tests, you already know that current averages are lower than historical averages. Thus, you must alter your assumptions about an acceptable volume, as well as about the likelihood of breakeven or profitable volume levels. It may be necessary to allow for a changing trend by using a weighted average. We will see later in this chapter how to apply this technique.

For now, let's concentrate on steps 2 and 3. First, you can broaden the dependability of your analysis by more specifically identifying possible outcomes. Second, you can use a shortcut method to identify percentages of likelihood that a desired result will be achieved. With this technique, you can estimate probability during a meeting, just with the use of a hand calculator.

In the case of two regions and nine groupings of possible outcomes, it was fairly easy to figure out how many events could occur. There were

45. But what if your tests were conducted on four regions and involved 15 likely results? It would take a long time to figure out the number of events that could occur.

Two formulas, for permutations and combinations, are helpful in determining the number of possible events. But before introducing them, we need to examine the use of factorials, because both formulas depend on them. A **factorial** is a total calculated by multiplying all the whole numbers between 1 and the number in question. For example, the factorial of 5 is 120:

$$1 \times 2 \times 3 \times 4 \times 5 = 120$$

The factorial is summarized in formulas by following the subject number with an exclamation point:

$$5! = 120$$

----

factorial—the total derived for any subject number by multiplying all whole numbers between 1 and the subject number.

Factorials are used to quickly calculate the number of possible ways that outcomes can occur given the number of factors involved and the number of arrangements. For example, the product test involved nine distinct factors (outcome groupings) and two arrangements (an outcome for each of two regions).

PERMUTATIONS

A **permutation** is the number of *different* outcomes, regardless of the order of occurrence. For example, the first region might end up with a 5 outcome and the second with a 6 outcome, or a 5-6. If the order is reversed so that the first region has a 6 and the second has a 5, that's a different outcome. Another rule of permutations is: THE SAME RESULT IN DIFFERENT GROUPINGS IS NOT COUNTED. For example, a 5-5 or a 6-6 outcome is not considered a permutation.

----

permutation—the number of different ways an outcome may occur, regardless of the order of occurrence.

With these considerations in mind, you must adjust the formula for a permutation to suit the test you are conducting. The permutation formula is shown in Figure 5-3. This formula states: THE NUMBER OF FACTORS (n) FOR A GIVEN NUMBER OF ARRANGEMENTS (r) IS EQUAL TO THE FACTORIAL OF n DIVIDED BY THE FACTORIAL FOR THE DIFFERENCE BETWEEN n AND r.

This is not as confusing as it may sound. When applied to the example of product testing, your probability analysis is based on 9 divisions of outcomes (number of factors, or n) and 2 regions (number of arrangements, or r). The formula is:

$$^9P_2 = \frac{9!}{(9 - 2)!}$$

Figure 5-3. Permutations.

$$^nP_r = \frac{n!}{(n-r)!}$$

n = number of factors
P = permutations
r = number of
     arrangements
! = factorial

The factorial of 2 is 2:

$$1 \times 2 = 2$$

And the factorial of 9 is 362,880:

$$1 \times 2 \times 3 \times 4 \times 5 \times 6 \times 7 \times 8 \times 9 = 362{,}880$$

We also need to compute the factorial of 7 for the value in the denominator, 9 minus 2:

$$1 \times 2 \times 3 \times 4 \times 5 \times 6 \times 7 = 5{,}040$$

The formula is simplified to read:

$$^{9}P_2 = \frac{362{,}880}{5{,}040}$$

The answer is 72. This is different from the answer in previous examples because in those we did not distinguish between reversed answers, like 5-6 and 6-5. The permutation recognizes these as two separate outcomes. In addition, we counted 5-5 and 6-6 as possible outcomes, whereas the permutation formula does not count identical results. We need to reconcile to a total of 45 for our example of product testing. The formula is a helpful shortcut, but it doesn't specifically suit our requirements.

To arrive at 45, we must make two adjustments. First, one-half of the 72 possible permutations must be excluded. These represent reversals of outcomes that were not counted as part of our test:

2-1	7-2	8-4
3-1	8-2	9-4
4-1	9-2	6-5
5-1	4-3	7-5
6-1	5-3	8-5
7-1	6-3	9-5
8-1	7-3	7-6
9-1	8-3	8-6
3-2	9-3	9-6
4-2	5-4	8-7
5-2	6-4	9-7
6-2	7-4	9-8

You will note that the total excluded cuts the answer in half, from 72 to 36.

The second adjustment it to add in the double results we recognized as possible outcomes:

1-1	4-4	7-7
2-2	5-5	8-8
3-3	6-6	9-9

We can now reconcile the formula for permutations with the list developed in Chapter 4:

Total developed by formula	72
Less: reverse-order outcomes	− 36
	36
Plus: duplicate outcomes	+ 9
	45

We can modify the formula for permutation to duplicate the total we came up with:

$$^nP_r = \left[\frac{n!}{(n-r)!} \times .5 \right] + n$$

The two adjustments work in all cases, making the formula valid. The permutation is first multiplied by .5, the same as dividing it by 2. The number of factors is then added. Substituting the symbols with the numbers in question, we have:

$$^9P_2 = \left[\frac{9!}{(9-2)!} \times .5 \right] + 9$$

$$= \left[\frac{362,880}{5,040} \times .5 \right] + 9$$

$$= \left[72 \times .5 \right] + 9$$

$$= 45$$

If the standard permutation formula has to be modified, you might ask, What good is it? It is useful in circumstances in which the permutation is the correct answer, without making the changes shown above. In our example, however, we needed to eliminate duplicate answers. In other instances, no such changes are needed.

Example: You have 2 job openings in your department, and 9 candidates have applied. No one employee may hold two jobs at the same time (eliminating the possibility of double outcomes like 5-5 and 6-6). However, reversals of outcomes, like 1-2 and 2-1 are possible. The permutation formula will produce the right answer:

$$^9P_2 = \frac{9!}{(9-2)!}$$

$$= 72$$

There are 72 possible permutations, or outcomes, to your decision.

Example: Ten salespeople are finalists in your company's ongoing sales contest. Only the top 4 will win prizes, awarded on total volume generated within a specified number of days. There will be no ties; only one person can win each of the 4 spots. The permutation formula tells how many possible ways the contest can end up in this case, because there can be no duplicate results, and reverse outcomes are possible:

$$^{10}P_4 = \frac{10!}{(10-4)!}$$

$$= \frac{3,628,800}{720}$$

$$= 5,040$$

There are 5,040 possible outcomes to the sales contest.

The permutation formula will apply in many business decisions. But in order to use it appropriately, you must first understand what the answer will include and exclude: all possible outcome sequences, but no duplicate outcomes.

COMBINATIONS

The outcome count is somewhat different when the reverse order doesn't count. A **combination** formula is closer to the one used in our example of two regions and nine groupings, because it does not count reverse-sequence outcomes like 5-6 and 6-5. Only one of those can apply in a combination. However, this formula does exclude duplicate outcomes such as 5-5 and 5-6, in the same way that the permutation formula does.

----

combination—the number of different arrangements of outcomes when the order of occurrence is not interchangeable.

The formula for a combination is summarized in Figure 5-4. Note the difference from permutation: The denominator is multiplied by the number of arrangements. This formula states: THE NUMBER OF FACTORS (*n*) FOR A GIVEN NUMBER OF ARRANGEMENTS (*r*) IS EQUAL TO THE FACTORIAL OF *n* DIVIDED BY THE PRODUCT OF THE FACTORIAL TIMES THE FACTORIAL OF

Figure 5-4.   Combinations.

$$^{n}C_{r} = \frac{n!}{r!(n-r)!}$$

n = **number of factors**
C = **combinations**
r = **number of arrangements**
! = **factorial**

r TIMES THE FACTORIAL OF THE DIFFERENCE BETWEEN n AND r. Using the product test example, we find:

$$^9C_2 = \frac{9!}{2!(9-2)!}$$

$$= \frac{362,880}{2 \times 5,040}$$

$$= 36$$

Because the combination formula does not include double outcomes like 5-5 and 6-6, we must modify the formula to arrive at the correct answer, 45:

$$^nC_r = \frac{n!}{r!(n-r)!} + n$$

Applying this revised formula to the example, we obtain:

$$^9C_2 = \frac{9!}{9!(9-2)!} + 9$$

$$= \frac{362,880}{2 \times 5,040} + 9$$

$$= 45$$

The combination formula works in many applications. You will need to remember exactly what the combination represents: possible combinations without reverse orders and no duplicate outcomes like 5-5 or 6-6.

Example: You have been given the task of completing a project and must select your team of four people from eight members of the department. The combination formula is applicable to this project because no one person can fill either of two spots (eliminating the chances of duplicate outcomes), and reversed outcomes won't count. The number of combinations possible is:

$$^8C_4 = \frac{8!}{4!(8-4)!}$$

$$= \frac{40,320}{24 \times 24}$$

$$= 70$$

There are 70 possible combinations for your project team.

Example: You presented a report to management suggesting a change in internal procedures. The proposed change addressed 11 areas of operations that would be affected by the change, each of which involved the potential for increased profits. The point made in your plan was that if any 3 of the 11 areas did not produce increased profits as a result of the change, the cost of the change would be justified. What are the number of possible combinations?

$$^{11}C_3 = \frac{11!}{3!(11-3)!}$$

$$= \frac{39,916,800}{6 \times 40,320}$$

$$= 165$$

There are 165 possible combinations that will produce the profitable mix mentioned in your report.

You can figure out the permutations and combinations of many questions involving probabilities. Even during a business meeting, you can quickly define variability and likely outcomes by applying these formulas.

Example: In a preliminary discussion of your product testing analysis, the president of the company asks you to provide a rough idea of results. You quickly figure out that there are 45 possible combinations for the 9 groups already defined. Knowing that the fifth group is in the middle, you can easily count the number of outcomes totaling 9, 10, and 11 (average middle-range outcomes for two regions and nine groups, as computed in Chapter 4). There are 13:

Total of 9 = 1-8, 2-7, 3-6, 4-5
Total of 10 = 1-9, 2-8, 3-7, 4-6, 5-5
Total of 11 = 2-9, 3-8, 4-7, 5-6

After you divide the total, 13, by 45, you can respond, "There is a 28.9 percent chance that the product will test at average levels."

This assumes, of course, that you have already established the dependability of the information used to (1) define the nine groups, (2) identify breakeven as it applies today, and (3) establish and agree upon what is an "acceptable" outcome to the product tests.

EXPECTATION VALUE

Broad-based testing improves the dependability of the raw data used in your probability analysis. Being able to quickly figure out permutations or combinations and respond appropriately—even during a meeting—is an enviable advantage.

Be aware, though, that even broad-based testing cannot always produce the best possible raw data. You will want to modify your hypothesis to allow for trends observed during testing.

----

expectation value—an average developed from observation of a number of random variable experiments.

Example: The nine outcome groupings developed for your probability analysis were based on historical averages for 800 products your company has developed. This was the test of random variables. However, you are also aware that the average first-week sales have been dropping during recent years. From this, you conclude that the average of past product sales volume is not adequate. You need to develop an **expectation value** based on your observations.

There are a number of ways to achieve this. One is to plot the trend and try to anticipate its rate. There is no assurance, however, that the rate of decline will continue or modify.

Another method is to define expectation value through the use of a weighted average. You begin with a summary of products marketed during every other year for the past two decades. The products selected are close to the average for all products marketed during the same year. Your list is:

Years on Market	Units Sold First Week
20	2,672
18	1,915
16	2,006
14	2,595
12	1,811
10	1,684
8	1,619
6	1,586
4	1,474
2	1,586
Total	18,948

Weight the average by adding one point for each declining two-year period. Thus, the oldest information (20 years) will have a weighted value of 1, and the latest will have a weighted value of 10:

Years on Market	Units Sold First Week		Weight		Total
20	2,672	×	1	=	2,672
18	1,915	×	2	=	3,830
16	2,006	×	3	=	6,018
14	2,595	×	4	=	10,380
12	1,811	×	5	=	9,055
10	1,684	×	6	=	10,104
8	1,619	×	7	=	11,333
6	1,586	×	8	=	12,688
4	1,474	×	9	=	13,266
2	1,586	×	10	=	15,860
Total	18,948				95,206

Figure 5-5.   Expectation value.

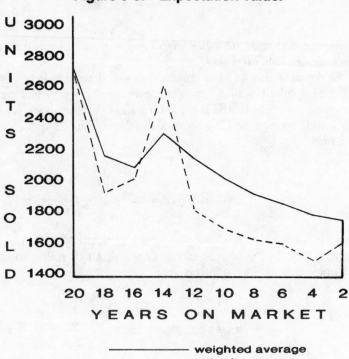

The results of expectation value are summarized in Figure 5-5. To derive this, first compute the weighted annual average which is currently 1,731 units:

$$\frac{95,206}{55} = 1,731$$

The weighted average for each period is computed by dividing the total accumulated to each period by the accumulated weight value to that point. For example, the third average is computed by adding the first three values and dividing the total by the accumulated weight (1 + 2 + 3, or a total of 6):

$$\frac{2,672 + 3,830 + 6,018}{6} = 2,087$$

Each average is entered on a line graph and compared with the actual number of units sold each year.

The dependability of your conclusions will depend largely on how valid your hypothesis is under current conditions. So a weighted average giving greater weight to the latest information may be more valuable than a simple average. In Chapter 6, we see how this technique can be carried further.

WORK PROJECT

1. Your department logged varying hours of overtime last year. You want to identify the degree of variation as part of your budget for the coming year. The record is:

Quarter	Overtime Hours
1	37
2	46
3	29
4	26

   a. Add and average the square of each quarter's hours.
   b. Subtract the square of the mean from the answer to item a above.
   c. Find the square root of the answer to item b above.
   d. Divide the answer in item c above by the mean.
   e. How many hours of variation from the average have you experienced in department overtime?
   f. What is the percentage of variation?
2. You are compiling an analysis of transactions processed, project requirements, and new positions in several departments as part of

a company-wide conversion budget. Part of your report will include probability analyses for:

- 8 possible ranges of transactions in 5 departments
- A pool of 9 available employees for a project team with 3 members
- 7 job openings to fill from an estimated 6 likely candidates for each position

As a preliminary step in your report:

a. Compute the factorial for:

```
Transactions:  8 _____
               5 _____
Project team:  9 _____
               3 _____
Job openings:  7 _____
               6 _____
```

b. Compute the number of permutations for each of the three studies, using the permutation formula:

$$_nP_r = \frac{n!}{(n-r)!}$$

Transactions _____
Project team _____
Job openings _____,

c. Compute the number of combinations for each of the three studies, using the combination formula:

$$_nC_r = \frac{n!}{r!\,(n-r)!}$$

Transactions _____
Project team _____
Job openings _____

3. Your department has been receiving a growing number of calls from customers. You are preparing a budget for the coming year and want to estimate requirements for additional phone lines and staff. Because the volume of calls has been growing, you know that expectation value is higher than the average. You summarize the number of calls per month for the past year:

Month	Calls	Month	Calls
Jan	103	Jul	133
Feb	118	Aug	172
Mar	109	Sep	113
Apr	126	Oct	155
May	182	Nov	162
Jun	121	Dec	149

Prepare a weighted average summary and show each month's totals. Remember the method for computing each period's weighted average: Divide accumulated weighted value as of each period by accumulated weight value to the same point. Use the chart below.

Month	Calls	Weight	Total	Weighted Average
Jan	_____	_____	_____	_____
Feb	_____	_____	_____	_____
Mar	_____	_____	_____	_____
Apr	_____	_____	_____	_____
May	_____	_____	_____	_____
Jun	_____	_____	_____	_____
Jul	_____	_____	_____	_____
Aug	_____	_____	_____	_____
Sep	_____	_____	_____	_____
Oct	_____	_____	_____	_____
Nov	_____	_____	_____	_____
Dec	_____	_____	_____	_____
Total	_____		_____	

6
Forecasting Techniques

Most statistical research goes wrong or becomes biased right at the beginning, in the way it is set up. It may set us up, too.

—Mark A. Johnson

Two managers were taking a course in basic statistics. After an evening in class, one said to the other, "I've noticed that every time a new idea is introduced, I have to look up three or four words just to make sense out of the idea. Why do statisticians obfuscate their message with so much terminology? Why can't they simplify it instead?"

The second manager replied, "I'll tell you, but only after I find out what 'obfuscate' means."

Forecasting a future outcome would be a simple matter if business problems contained only one possible event. The test of success or failure, profit or loss, and achieving or not achieving a specific volume level could be easily reduced to a matter of black and white. But, in fact, you rarely face simple questions having one positive or one negative answer. It's much more likely that the questions you need to answer will have many dimensions and qualifications.

Even the seemingly easy questions may go beyond the most obvious response. For example, you may be asked these questions today or tomorrow:

- Will you have an unfavorable variance in your departmental budget?

- Will the variance be greater than 5 percent of the amount estimated?
- Will you be able to reverse the negative trend those budget results show?

The answer to any of these cannot be a simple yes or no. Chances are, your answer will have to begin with the phrase "That depends."

You have already seen how a sample can be used to test a larger body of information—the population. If the sample is fair, it will tell you how that population is likely to act. You can apply this idea to forecasting. But, when you confront a combination of different events, the problem becomes more complicated—just as the outcome from rolling two six-sided dice is far more complicated than tossing a single coin. In most of your forecasting tasks, you will need to test your samples with more advanced techniques.

A COMBINATION OF EVENTS

When you are forecasting the future, you don't just face the question of whether or not a year-long total is accurate. Your forecast is predicated on a series of events taking place, and the accuracy of that forecast rests on the accuracy of your assumptions.

Example: You are the marketing director for an engineering consulting firm. Your six-month forecast of gross revenue is based on the following assumptions:

1. During the six-month period, a total of eight projects will be put out for bid.
2. Your firm will win two of these projects.

In this case, you are working with two assumptions: Eight projects will be put out for bid, and your firm will win 25 percent of those projects.

The accuracy of your prediction depends not only on historical outcomes (the percentage of bids won, for example) but also on the volume of new bids coming onto the market. Thus, even if your firm does maintain its historical average, what is the probability that there will be more bids on the market. Or fewer bids? There are two variables at work.

When your forecast involves a number of different events, you have to allow for the possibility of variation within each event. For example, next year's sales may vary because of changes in a number of areas: the number of salespeople recruited, the number of people who resign, average sales volume, economic conditions, the competition, and the quality of sales leadership in remote branch offices, for example. The formulas used for this level of estimating involve the use of factorials, which were introduced in Chapter 5.

The factorial of a number, you will recall, is the product of all whole numbers between 1 and the number itself. Thus, the factorial of 3 is:

$$1 \times 2 \times 3 = 6$$

Below is a table of the factorials for values zero through 12. Note the factorial for zero is always equal to 1.

Factorials

0 =	1
1 =	1
2 =	2
3 =	6
4 =	24
5 =	120
6 =	720
7 =	5,040
8 =	40,320
9 =	362,880
10 =	3,628,800
11 =	39,916,800
12 =	479,001,600

We will use a shorthand factorial expression to make the formulas for estimating less involved. When a value or symbol is placed above another and enclosed in parentheses, it signifies the formula for a combination. This abbreviated factorial expression is shown in Figure 6-1.

DISTRIBUTION FOR TWO VARIABLE FACTORS

The first formula involving a combination of events is called a **binomial distribution.** This equation shows the percentage of probability for questions in which the outcome depends on two factors—for example, the assumption that your firm will win 25 percent of the bids available during the next 6 months, based on the related assumption that 8 bids will come up.

----

binomial distribution—the distribution of values derived when a combination of events occurs in a series of probability trials.

Continuing with the example of forecasting revenue for the engineering consulting company, there will be an estimated 8 projects, of

Figure 6-1. Factorial expression.

$$\binom{n}{r} = \frac{n!}{r!(n-r)!}$$

n = range of responses
r = responses
! = factorial

which you believe your company will win 2. The formula for the binomial distribution has three sections:

1. The combinations you are likely to experience (8 bids, of which your company expects to win 2)
2. The likelihood that an event *will* take place (winning 2 projects)
3. The likelihood that an event *will not* take place (not winning 6 projects)

The first part of this equation identifies the number of combinations possible to achieve this outcome:

$$\frac{8!}{2! \, (8-2)!}$$

This may also be abbreviated with the use of the shortcut factorial expression:

$$\binom{8}{2}$$

The second part of the equation expresses the probability of achieving the 25 percent goal. (Remember that the first part only identifies possible combinations of outcomes—the number of chances that 8 projects will come up for bid and that your firm will win 2 of those jobs.) In this case, you expect to win 2 bids; so there will be 2 trials. Overall, you believe you will win one-fourth, or 25 percent, of the projects bid (two out of eight). It isn't accurate to merely state that you have a one-in-four chance of getting the desired outcome. Each possible outcome (a won bid) has a 25 percent chance of occurring. So the real probability is 25 percent that *each* outcome will occur. Thus, the probability has to be raised to its second power (for each of the two outcomes):

$$.25^2 = (.25 \times .25) = .06250$$

The third section deals with the likelihood that 6 out of the 8 projects will *not* be won. Or, expressed in another way, each outcome has a three-in-four chance of not occurring. If *1* is the value of all outcomes, this likelihood is:

$$1 - .25 = .75$$

Out of a total of 8 outcomes, the probability of not winning a project 6 times is summarized as:

$$(1 - .25)^{8-2}$$

This statement can be reduced to the expression:

$$.75^6$$

You can now put the 3 sections of the formula together:

1. Possible combinations
2. Chance of events occurring
3. Chance of events not occurring

The formula for binomial distribution multiplies each of these 3 parts together (see Figure 6-2).

Figure 6-2.   Binomial distribution.

$$\Pr(x=r) = \binom{n}{r} \, p^r \, (1-p)^{n-r}$$

Pr = probability
x = outcome
r = response
n = number of trials
p = degree of probability

After we combine the three parts, the formula states: The probability that we will win 2 projects equals (1) the number of combinations of 2 out of 8 events times (2) the chances of winning 2 projects times (3) the chances of not winning 6 projects. Replacing the symbols with the values in the example, we have:

Number of trials (n) = 8
Degree of probability (p) = .25
Projects won (r) = 2

And substituting these values in the formula gives:

$$Pr(x = 2) = \frac{8!}{2!(8-2)!} .25^2 (1-.25)^{8-2}$$

$$= \frac{40,320}{2(720)} .06250 (.75)^6$$

$$= \frac{40,320}{1,440} .06250 (.17798)$$

$$= 28 \times .06250 \times .17798$$

$$= .311$$

There is a 31.1 percent chance that the outcome in your forecast will come to pass. You may ask, "Why do I have to change the probability for the number of responses?" Remember that the higher the possible number of outcomes you are likely to see, the lower your chances for complete success. For example, if you toss a coin once, there is a 50-50 chance (a probability of .50) that heads will come up. A second toss has the same independent probability; but the probability of *both* tosses coming up heads is only 25 percent (probability of $.50^2$, or .25). The probability of three tosses all coming up heads is $.50^3$, or .125:

$$.50^3 = (.50 \times .50 \times .50) = .125$$

Below is a series of tables of the degree of probability for outcomes between 5 and 95 percent, up to the tenth power, that you may use for calculating binomial distribution for additional problems in this chapter:

Power	$P = .05$	$P = .10$	$P = .15$	$P = .20$	$P = .25$
1	.05000	.10000	.15000	.20000	.25000
2	.00250	.01000	.02250	.04000	.06250
3	.00013	.00100	.00338	.00800	.01563
4	.00001	.00010	.00051	.00160	.00391
5	.00000	.00001	.00008	.00032	.00098
6		.00000	.00001	.00006	.00024
7			.00000	.00001	.00006
8				.00000	.00002
9					.00000
10					

Power	$P = .30$	$P = .35$	$P = .40$	$P = .45$	$P = .50$
1	.30000	.35000	.40000	.45000	.50000
2	.09000	.12250	.16000	.20250	.25000
3	.02700	.04287	.06400	.09113	.12500
4	.00810	.01501	.02560	.04101	.06250
5	.00243	.00525	.01024	.01845	.03125
6	.00073	.00184	.00410	.00830	.01563
7	.00022	.00064	.00164	.00374	.00781
8	.00007	.00023	.00066	.00168	.00391
9	.00002	.00008	.00026	.00076	.00195
10	.00001	.00003	.00010	.00034	.00098

Power	$P = .55$	$P = .60$	$P = .65$	$P = .70$	$P = .75$
1	.55000	.60000	.65000	.70000	.75000
2	.30250	.36000	.42250	.49000	.56250
3	.16638	.21600	.27463	.34300	.42188
4	.09151	.12960	.17851	.24010	.31641
5	.05033	.07776	.11603	.16807	.23730
6	.02768	.04666	.07542	.11765	.17798
7	.01522	.02799	.04902	.08235	.13348
8	.00837	.01680	.03186	.05765	.10011
9	.00461	.01008	.02071	.04035	.07508
10	.00253	.00605	.01346	.02825	.05631

Power	P = .80	P = .85	P = .90	P = .95
1	.80000	.85000	.90000	.95000
2	.64000	.72250	.81000	.90250
3	.51200	.61413	.72900	.85738
4	.40960	.52201	.65610	.81451
5	.32768	.44371	.59049	.77378
6	.26214	.37715	.53144	.73509
7	.20972	.32058	.47830	.69834
8	.16777	.27249	.43047	.66342
9	.13422	.23162	.38742	.63025
10	.10737	.19687	.34868	.59874

THE VISUAL PROBABILITY

When you calculate binomial distribution with an equally spaced range of possible outcomes, you get a normal distribution. That means the distribution has a bell-shaped curve with the same dimensions on both sides. But, in fact, distribution is not always quite as symmetrical. The real values of one side or the other in the curve often vary. This variance is called the **density function.**

---

density function—the degree of probability that a random variable will have a specific value.

Example: You want to express the probability of responses to a customer survey. There are two possible outcomes: Customers will complete the survey and return it, or they will not. Even though you will send the survey to thousands of customers, your test will be performed on the basis of responses from ten people.

To chart the density function of successes (positive responses), the binomial distribution formula is calculated ten times. In each case, the number of trials (n) is 10. But the response (r) varies:

$$r = 1 \qquad r = 6$$
$$r = 2 \qquad r = 7$$
$$r = 3 \qquad r = 8$$
$$r = 4 \qquad r = 9$$
$$r = 5 \qquad r = 10$$

There are ten possible outcomes, one for each response. The binomial distribution factors for these ten outcomes will produce a symmetrical curve. Use the probability table in the previous section to help in your calculations:

$$\Pr(x=1) = \frac{10!}{1!(10-1)!} \, .50^1 \, (1-.50)^{10-1}$$

$$= \frac{3,628,800}{1(362,880)} \, .50 \, (.0020)$$

$$= .010$$

$$\Pr(x=2) = \frac{10!}{2!(10-2)!} \, .50^2 \, (1-.50)^{10-2}$$

$$= .044$$

$$\Pr(x=3) = \frac{10!}{3!(10-3)!} \, .50^3 \, (1-.50)^{10-3}$$

$$= .117$$

$$\Pr(x=4) = \frac{10!}{4!(10-4)!} \, .50^4 \, (1-.50)^{10-4}$$

$$= .205$$

$$\Pr(x=5) = \frac{10!}{5!(10-5)!} \, .50^5 \, (1-.50)^{10-5}$$

$$= .246$$

$$\Pr(x=6) = \frac{10!}{6!(10-6)!} \, .50^6 \, (1-.50)^{10-6}$$

$$= .205$$

$$\Pr(x=7) = \frac{}{7!(10-7)!} \cdot .50^7 \, (1-.50)^{10-7}$$

$$= .117$$

$$\Pr(x=8) = \frac{10!}{8!(10-8)!} \cdot .50^8 \, (1-.50)^{10-8}$$

$$= .044$$

$$\Pr(x=9) = \frac{10!}{9!(10-9)!} \cdot .50^9 \, (1-.50)^{10-9}$$

$$= .010$$

$$\Pr(x=10) = \frac{10!}{6!(10-10)!} \cdot .50^{10} \, (1-50)^{10-10}$$

$$= .001$$

The percentage of responses can be reduced to the density function for responses 0 through 10. A response of zero is identical to a response of 10:

Response	Probability	Percent
r = 0	.001	0.1%
r = 1	.010	1.0
r = 2	.044	4.4
r = 3	.117	11.7
r = 4	.205	20.5
r = 5	.246	24.6
r = 6	.205	20.5
r = 7	.117	11.7
r = 8	.044	4.4
r = 9	.010	1.0
r = 10	.001	0.1

The density function graph in Figure 6-3 shows the range of outcomes in symmetrical order.

Figure 6-3.   Binomial density function (example 1).

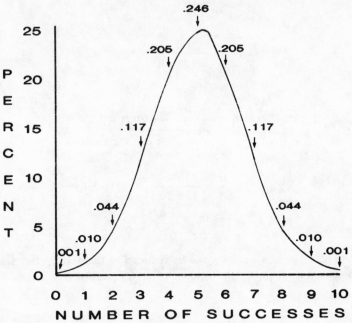

This formula can be applied to a number of business situations. Start out by first calculating the probability for outcome.

Example: One of the employees in your department has been attending a company-sponsored class to improve job-related skills. A ten-question examination consisting of true or false responses will be given at the end of the week. In a discussion with your employee, you discover that he is having difficulty with the material. He needs to have no less than six correct answers to pass, and he asks you, "What are my chances of guessing six out of ten of the questions correctly?"

Although you would prefer that your employee learn the material so that guessing wouldn't be necessary, you can use the binomial distribution formula to figure out the probability. The number of trials (questions) is 10. The probability for each is 50 percent (true or false answer). And the required number of correct responses is 6:

$$n = 10$$
$$p = .50$$
$$r = 6$$

Recalling the formula for binomial distribution, we have:

$$\Pr (x = 6) = \frac{10!}{6!(10-6)!} .50^6 (1 - .50)^{10-6}$$

$$= \frac{3,628,800}{720(24)} .01563 (.50)^4$$

$$= 210 \times .01563 \times .06250$$

$$= .205$$

Your employee has a 20.5 percent chance of guessing six answers correctly. Another way to express this is that the chances of passing the test are 79.5 percent *against* guessing correctly. With this information, perhaps the employee can be encouraged to study so that the probability of passing the exam will be improved.

This chance of success—about one in five—is much different from what a lot of people would assume given the facts. Because each question is either true or false, there's a 50-50 chance of guessing correctly. But remember, that 50-50 chance applies to all ten questions. Thus, guessing two correctly has greater odds than just guessing one correctly. This is why the odds are very much against passing the test purely by guesswork.

Example: Reports are prepared in draft form and then sent to the word processing pool for final version. You will submit an estimated ten reports over the next ten weeks. Of the five employees in the pool, three are known for their accuracy and correct spelling; the other two tend to make a lot of mistakes. Work in the pool is assigned on a random basis.

What is the probability that your work will be assigned to one of the three dependable employees in four of the next ten weeks?

To compute this probability, it is first necessary to figure out the percentage of desired responses. Out of 5 employees, 3, or 60 percent, are dependable:

$$\tfrac{3}{5} = 60\%$$

The number of total trials (weeks) is 10. The degree of probability during each week is 60 percent (.60). The number of weeks being tested is 4:

$$n = 10$$
$$p = .60$$
$$r = 4$$

To determine the probability that your work will go to one of the three dependable employees in the word processing pool in four of the next ten weeks:

$$\Pr(x = 4) = \frac{10!}{4!(10-4)!} \, .60^4 \, (1 - .60)^{10-4}$$

$$= \frac{3,628,800}{24(720)} \, .12960 \, (.40)^6$$

$$= 210 \times .12960 \times .00410$$

$$= .112$$

There is an 11.2 percent probability that your work will go to one of the three dependable employees in four of the next ten weeks.

The curve, or density function, for this probability won't be symmetrical. The number of weeks being tested and the number of successful outcomes are dissimilar; so the curve will rise and fall at an unbalanced rate. If you calculate binomial distribution for each of the ten weeks, your results will be:

Response	Probability	Percent
r = 1	.002	0.2
r = 2	.011	1.1
r = 3	.043	4.3
r = 4	.112	11.2
r = 5	.200	20.0
r = 6	.251	25.1
r = 7	.215	21.5
r = 8	.121	12.1
r = 9	.040	4.0
r = 10	.006	0.6

When this distribution is expressed on a density function chart, the pattern will look like that shown in Figure 6-4.

MORE THAN ONE COMBINATION

You may face the problem of having to compute the outcome for a combination of combinations. The calculation with the formidable title **hypergeometric distribution** is used for such a calculation.

With this formula, your task is to figure out the number of possible combinations for two possible outcomes and divide that number by the total number of overall outcomes. When a sample is taken from a population, the question being asked is, "What is the probability that a specified number of outcomes will occur?"

---

hypergeometric distribution—the probability that a sample drawn from a population will contain a specified number of assumed outcomes.

Example: The president of your company recently announced that five openings were available in another division. Nine people applied for these openings, including two from your department. What is the

Figure 6-4.   Binomial density function (example 2).

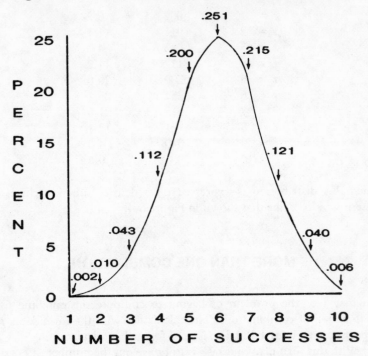

probability that both of your employees will be included among the five selected? Or, asking the question in a different manner, what is the probability that of the five people selected, three will be from other departments?

This formula uses the shortcut factorial expression explained earlier in this chapter. It is a series of combinations:

- There are $\binom{7}{3}$ ways to select seven people for three positions (nine applicants less the two from your department).

- There are $\binom{2}{2}$ ways to select two people for the other two positions.

- There are $\binom{9}{5}$ possible selections overall.

Expressed as a formula, the probability is:

$$\Pr(x=3) = \frac{\binom{7}{3}\ \binom{2}{2}}{\binom{9}{5}}$$

The factorial expression is an abbreviated version of a series of combinations. The longer version of this is:

$$\frac{\left(\dfrac{7!}{3!(7-3)!}\right)\ \left(\dfrac{2!}{2!(2-2)!}\right)}{\left(\dfrac{9!}{5!(9-5)!}\right)}$$

Computing the outcome, we obtain:

$$= \frac{\left(\dfrac{5{,}040}{6(24)}\right)\ \left(\dfrac{2}{2(1)}\right)}{\left(\dfrac{362{,}880}{120(24)}\right)}$$

$$= \frac{(35)\ \ (1)}{126}$$

$$= \frac{35}{126}$$

$$= 27.8\%$$

There is a 27.8 percent chance that the two employees in your department will be included in the five selected. There are 126 possible combinations of 5 among the 9 applicants. And of that number, 35 include the 2 employees in your department.

With a formula this complex, how can you prove that the answer is correct? The formula states that there are 126 possible combinations, and that of those, your 2 employees have a 27.8 percent chance of being included, or 35 out of 126 trials. Although this is a fairly large number of combinations, it can be proved by listing all of the possible ways that five people can be selected.

If we assume that the applicants are assigned numbers 1 through 9, the combinations can be listed in sequence. You can further assume that your employees are applicants 1 and 2 (or any other two numbers). After the combinations are listed, count those that include both 1s and 2s. The possible combinations are:

12345	12469	13478	14689	23579	34567
12346	12478	13479	14789	23589	34568
12347	12479	13489	15678	23678	34569
12348	12489	13567	15679	23679	34578
12349	12567	13568	15689	23689	34579
12356	12568	13569	15789	23789	34589
12357	12569	13578	16789	24567	34678
12358	12578	13579	23456	24568	34679
12359	12579	13589	23457	24569	34689
12367	12589	13678	23458	24578	34789
12368	12678	13679	23459	24579	35678
12369	12679	13689	23467	24589	35679
12378	12689	13789	23468	24678	35689
12379	12789	14567	23469	24679	35789
12389	13456	14568	23478	24689	36789
12456	13457	14569	23479	24789	45678
12457	13458	14578	23489	25678	45679
12458	13459	14579	23567	25679	45689
12459	13467	14589	23568	25689	45789
12467	13468	14678	23569	25789	46789
12468	13469	14679	23578	26789	56789

This exercise establishes the fact that there are 126 possible 5-way combinations of the numbers 1 through 9. If you count the combinations containing numbers 1 and 2, you will discover that there are 35. The same number of possible combinations can be found for any two numbers you select.

The formula for hypergeometric distribution can be explained by the question: WHAT IS THE PROBABILITY (PR) THAT THE RANDOM VARIABLE (x) WILL EQUAL A SPECIFIED NUMBER OF SUCCESSES (A)? Applying this question to the example, we want to know, "What is the probability that of the nine people applying for five positions, three of those selected will be from other departments?" The answer to this question identifies the same probability that the two people from your department will be selected to fill the remaining two positions.

The formula can be expressed with symbols:

A = number of possible successes (7 out of 9)
a = number of outcomes for those successes (3 out of the 5 positions)
R = number of excluded outcomes (2 out of 9)
r = remaining outcomes (2 out of the 5 positions)
T = total field of selection (9 applicants)
t = number of selections (5 positions available)

Using these symbols, we arrive at the formula for hypergeometric distribution shown in Figure 6-5.

Example: An auditor examines 10 transactions in the books of your company. Of the 10, 6 involved amounts above $500 and four were for lower amounts. If the auditor subsequently selects random groupings of five transactions, what is the probability that each group will include three transactions above $500?

In this example, the formula consists of the following values:

a = 3 (selected transactions above $500)
r = 2 (selected transactions below $500)
A = 6 (number of transactions in previous test above $500)
R = 4 (number of transactions in previous test below $500)
T = 10 (total transactions in previous test)
t = 5 (total transactions in new test)

Figure 6-5. Hypergeometric distribution.

$$\Pr(x=a) = \frac{\binom{A}{a}\binom{R}{r}}{\binom{T}{t}}$$

Pr = probability
x = random variable
A = possible successes
a = number of successes
R = excluded outcomes
r = remaining outcomes
T = total field of selection
t = number of selections

The hypergeometric distribution formula for this example is:

$$\Pr(x=3) = \frac{\binom{6}{3}\binom{4}{2}}{\binom{10}{5}}$$

$$= \frac{\left(\frac{720}{6(6)}\right)\left(\frac{24}{2(2)}\right)}{\left(\frac{3,628,800}{120\,(120)}\right)}$$

$$= \frac{120}{252}$$

$$= 47.6\%$$

There is a 47.6 percent chance that three out of five transactions will be greater than $500.

The two forms of distribution in this chapter—binomial and hypergeometric—are both based on the assumption that variables are directly related to one another. For example, positive and negative outcomes equal the total likely outcomes. But when you estimate outcomes with unrelated variables, the task is more complicated. This is the topic of Chapter 7.

WORK PROJECT

1. You are preparing several formulas using factorials and factorial expressions:
    a. Write out the combinations represented by these factorial expressions:

    (1) $\begin{pmatrix} 10 \\ 6 \end{pmatrix}$

    (2) $\begin{pmatrix} 9 \\ 4 \end{pmatrix}$

    (3) $\begin{pmatrix} 7 \\ 2 \end{pmatrix}$

    b. Show the abbreviated factorial expressions for the following combinations:

(1) $\dfrac{6!}{2!(6-2)!}$

(2) $\dfrac{11!}{7!(11-7)!}$

(3) $\dfrac{8!}{2!(8-2)!}$

2. Compute the binomial distribution for the values below, using the formula:

$$Pr(x=r) = \binom{n}{r} p^r (1-p)^{n-r}$$

a. $r = 6$
   $n = 9$
   $p = .65$

b. $r = 7$
   $n = 10$
   $p = .80$

c. $r = 6$
   $n = 11$
   $p = .45$

3. Compute hypergeometric distribution for the values below, using the formula:

$$\dfrac{\binom{A}{a}\binom{R}{r}}{\binom{T}{t}}$$

a. $a = 3$
   $r = 2$
   $A = 4$
   $R = 3$
   $T = 7$
   $t = 5$

b. $a = 2$
   $r = 1$
   $A = 6$
   $R = 4$
   $T = 10$
   $t = 3$

c. $a = 3$
   $r = 1$
   $A = 5$
   $R = 3$
   $T = 8$
   $t = 4$

7

Testing the Accuracy of Forecasts

Mathematics, rightly viewed, possesses not only truth but supreme beauty—a beauty cold and austere, like that of sculpture.

—Bertrand Russell

"You've got a tough job ahead of you," the manager told the new employee in the research department. "Our president respected the guy you're replacing and had great faith in his forecasting abilities."

"Was he a statistician?" the employee asked.

"In a way. He used to hang around the lunchroom and read coffee grounds."

Although there is no magic involved in statistics, the task of forecasting does involve a combination of insight, estimation, luck, and science. Working with only one random variable, you need to identify probabilities to predict the most likely future outcome. When two random variables are involved, the estimate is more complex. You then need a different approach to statistical analysis, keeping in mind the variability of two separate values.

Fortunately, many events are noticeably related and do affect one another, often quite directly and in a predictable pattern. **Regression analysis** is the statistical name for the study of the relationships of two or more random variables. In some cases, two or more variables are completely independent. But in most cases, variables affect one another directly enough that a dependable prediction of each is possible.

IDENTIFYING THE STRAIGHT LINE

In business applications, there is often a very specific cause and effect between related values and events. Some examples are:

- An increase in sales volume changes the percentage of cost of goods sold, as well as levels of fixed overhead.
- The volume of sales closed is directly related to the number of calls a salesperson makes.
- Changes in market interest rates affect demand for homes, cars, and other consumer goods.
- The number of employees in your department influences your budget for many expenses, such as office supplies, telephone, and travel.

----

regression analysis—the study of the mathematical relationships between two or more variables.

You can visually analyze the relationship between variables by creating a graph showing the regression line. The formula for this line is shown in Figure 7-1.

Example: One of your suppliers charges you varying amounts for filling orders. The charge includes a $2 charge plus 5¢ per item.

Applying the regression line formula, we have:

$$a = 2.00$$
$$b = .05$$

Figure 7-1.   Regression line.

$$Y = a + bX$$

Y = dependent variable
a = fixed value a
b = fixed value b
X = independent variable

The formula will reveal the value of Y, the dependent variable. It is dependent because it is based on changes in the fixed values a and b. The independent variable, X, is the number of items ordered:

$$Y = 2.00 + .05X$$

If you order 125 items, X becomes 125:

$$
\begin{aligned}
Y &= 2.00 + .05(125) \\
&= 2.00 + 6.25 \\
&= 8.25
\end{aligned}
$$

The values a and b (2.00 and .05 in this example) are given the statistical name **coefficients,** or numbers by which a quantity will be multiplied. So in regression analysis, your task is to identify the value of the dependent Y, which is based on the independent variable X, when working with coefficients a and b.

----

coefficient—the number by which a quantity is to be multiplied.

The regression line for this example can be easily plotted on a diagram. However, the graph you use is different from the typical line graph, where value and time are shown on opposing axes. In this instance, the variables are placed vertically and horizontally, and each value is identified as an intersect.

Example: You already know that if you order 125 parts from your supplier, you will be charged $8.25. How much will you be charged if you order only 50 items?

$$Y = 2.00 + .05(50)$$
$$= 4.50$$

You now have two results: $8.25 for 125 items, and $4.50 for 50 items. You can now create a regression diagram (Figure 7-2). The top-to-

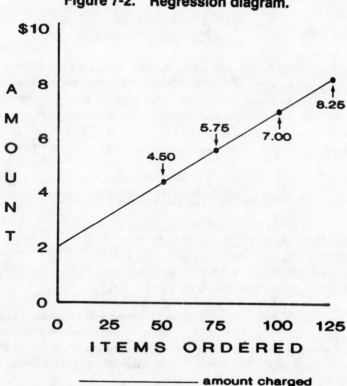

Figure 7-2.   Regression diagram.

bottom scale represents the amount, and the left-to-right scale shows the number of items ordered.

We know that $2 will always be charged for placing an order, so the straight line begins at that point. The variable in this instance is the number of items ordered. Note that the total amounts are written in for 50, 75, 100, and 125 orders. But we have computed the values only for the first and last quantities. This points out the value of regressive analysis. You need to identify only two dependable points, and, as long as the relationship involves a straight line, other values can be dependably worked out. To prove this point, perform the regression analysis for 75 and 100 items:

$$Y = 2.00 + .05(75)$$
$$= 5.75$$

$$Y = 2.00 + .05(100)$$
$$= 7.00$$

In this example, you can figure out the regression line because the coefficients are known values. You know the supplier will always charge $2 for placing an order, plus 5¢ for each item. When you aren't sure about the values of coefficients, creating a regression line will take a bit more work. However, the result will be the same: You will end up with a diagram showing the likely outcome at varying levels of activity.

ESTIMATING THE REGRESSION LINE

You can apply the principles of regression analysis to forecasting and budgeting. Here, you constantly look for trends, hoping to make as accurate a prediction as possible. Thus, you want to find the straight-line, or linear, relationship between values.

Example: You are working on a budget for telephone expenses. Looking at last year's totals, you notice that phone expenses were higher during the heavy-volume season. From this, you recognize a cause and effect between sales activity and telephone expenses. Your budget is based on changes in the sales forecast.

You do not know the precise value of future sales, nor of telephone expenses. However, your budget can be based on several logical assumptions:

- There is a direct relationship between sales activity and telephone expense.
- The same approximate relationship will continue in the future.
- The degree of change in the telephone budget can be approximated on the basis of the degree of change in sales volume.

All of these assumptions could be wrong, and all are dependent on estimates. So your task is first to decide whether the apparent relationship exists or is only coincidental. From there, you will have to judge the extent of cause and effect. In a budgeting situation, you may use guesswork more than science, and that's to be expected. A budget, after all, is nothing more than a general guideline, a series of broad assumptions against which actual results can be measured.

You can greatly simplify your task by using regression analysis. When you study the relationship between two related variables over time, you achieve these advantages:

- A likely future outcome based on a study of the relationship
- Identification of accuracy of your estimates, based on the degree of variability from the average

All of your statistical findings will be based on estimates and cannot be depended on as the last word. Your actual outcome will vary from your budget to some degree in the majority of accounts, because the future cannot be precisely measured. However, you can narrow the uncertainty of estimation with regressive analysis.

Example: You work for a consulting firm that bases its forecasting and budgeting on hours billed to clients. In the coming year, management plans to expand its consulting staff and client billings. Your task is to develop an expense budget. In summarizing past trends, you notice that as hours billed rise, overall expenses rise as well; and that when hours billed decline, so does the level of expenses.

Your initial concern is whether the apparent relationship between hours billed and monthly expenses is a coincidence or indicates the need for better expense controls, rather than mere acceptance of the trend. You eliminate the possibility that it's a coincidence, because the relationship can be observed over several years. And most of the variation of expense levels occurs in selling expenses, which are affected by the level of revenue-generating activity (including telephone, travel, entertainment, and advertising). You summarize results from the past year:

Month	Hours Billed	Monthly Expense ($00)
Jan	365	$ 96
Feb	357	94
Mar	424	111
Apr	381	105
May	362	95
Jun	405	110
Jul	406	109
Aug	392	111
Sep	365	100
Oct	417	112
Nov	394	107
Dec	352	98
Total	4,620	$1,248
Mean	385	$104

The mean (average) shows that 385 hours are billed in the average month, and $10,400 (104 × $100) is incurred in expenses. In some budgeting situations, this is the extent of trend analysis. A manager simply compares one mean with the other and applies that to the budget on the assumption that this relationship is a constant one:

$$\frac{104}{385} = 27\%$$

Thus, if future sales are forecast on the basis of hours billed, total expenses could be estimated at 27 percent of those levels. The problem, though, is that budgeting on the basis of a mean may not be very accurate.

An alternative is to estimate likely future levels by creating a **scatter diagram,** a graph in which values are identified by their intersect and a regression line is estimated from their average placement.

---

scatter diagram—a graph on which two variables are observed by placement of dots at intersect points and a regression line is drawn to approximate the trend.

In the example, you can observe the relationships of hours billed to monthly expenses and create a scatter diagram. For example, expense levels are listed from top to bottom, and hours billed from left to right. Intersect points of expenses and hours are then identified:

Jan	96–365
Feb	94–357
Mar	111–424

A dot is placed at each of the intersects for the entire year. The result is shown in Figure 7-3, with an estimate of average expense levels indicated by the line drawn through the field of dots.

The scatter diagram is useful as a general estimate of a trend. However, it is not precise enough for every situation you will face. If your budget is based on this technique, how, during a budget review meeting, will you answer such questions as "How accurate is this budget?" and "Where is your documentation supporting what it shows?"

Figure 7-3.   Scatter diagram.

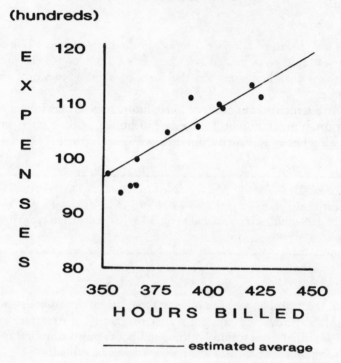

(hundreds)

estimated average

REDUCING THE DEVIATION

To add a bit more science to your estimate of future outcomes, you can use a technique called **least squares** to describe a trend. This method identifies points on a graph that represent the minimum degree of deviation from statistical averages.

----

least squares—a method of calculating a regression line using the sum of deviations squared; the sum represents the minimum degree of deviation from averages.

To calculate least squares, identify coefficients for the regression line formula by studying deviations in raw data. You will recall the formula:

$$Y = a + bX$$

The values of a and b, the coefficients, are based on a summary of squared deviations from the mean of the data. To start, create a table based on the values being used. In our example, we compared hours billed and monthly expense levels (in hundreds of dollars). Table 1 shows how these values are put to work. You use the previous year's data, compute the distance from the mean in each month, and figure out the square of those distances.

X = hours billed
Y = monthly expenses (in hundreds)
x = distance from the mean of X
y = distance from the mean of Y
x^2 = square of the distance from the mean of X
y^2 = square of the distance from the mean of y
xy = value of x multiplied by value of y

Table 1. Least squares computations.

Month	X	Y	x	y	x²	y²	xy
Jan	365	$ 96	−20	− 8	400	64	160
Feb	357	94	−28	−10	784	100	280
Mar	424	111	39	7	1,521	49	273
Apr	381	105	− 4	1	16	1	4
May	362	95	−23	− 9	529	81	207
Jun	405	110	20	6	400	36	120
Jul	406	109	21	5	441	25	105
Aug	392	111	7	7	49	49	49
Sep	365	100	−20	− 4	400	16	80
Oct	417	112	32	8	1,024	64	256
Nov	394	107	9	3	81	9	27
Dec	352	98	−33	− 6	1,089	36	198
Total	4,620	$1,248	0	0	6,734	530	1,759
Mean	385	$104					

Each of the columns shown in Table 1 will be used for the formulas covered in this chapter, as well as to develop a second table showing you how to measure deviation. Here's how the columns in Table 1 were created:

X: This is a duplication of monthly hours billed during the past year.

Y: This column is a summary of expenses per month in hundreds of dollars. Thus, the total of 1,248 represents \$124,800, and the mean (average) of 104 represents \$10,400.

x: This is the distance from the mean of X. January's total hours, 365, minus the mean, 385, is -20. The March total of 424 minus the mean, 385, is 39. The sum of distances from the mean always equals zero.

y: This is the distance from the mean of Y. The same calculation is performed here that applied for the previous column. Subtract the mean (104) from each month's total. The sum of distances, again, always equals zero.

x^2: This is the square of the distance x. Thus, the January x value of -20, when squared, equals 400:

$$-20 \times -20 = 400$$

y^2: This is the square of the distance y. Thus, the January y value of -8, when squared, equals 64:

$$-8 \times -8 = 64$$

xy: This column shows the value of x multiplied by the value of y. For example, January's x value is -20, and January's y value is -8:

$$-20 \times -8 = 160$$

These values are all shown as positives, even when negative distances are multiplied by positive distances. The concern here is not with the direction away from the mean, only with the value of the combined distance.

BUILDING THE DIAGRAM

From the information developed in Table 1, you can find the values of coefficients *a* and *b* for the regression line formula and create the regression diagram. The value of *b* is computed by dividing the total in the *xy* column by the total in the x^2 column:

$$b = \frac{xy}{x^2}$$

$$= \frac{1,759}{6,734}$$

$$= 0.2612$$

This coefficient, *b*, represents the incremental cost that varies according to the number of hours billed.

The value of *a* is computed by the following steps:

1. Multiply the total of X by the value of *b* (the total computed above).
2. Subtract that total from the total of Y.
3. Divide the remaining amount by *n*, the number of periods (in this example, $n = 12$ months).

The formula for *a* is:

$$a = \frac{Y - (Xb)}{n}$$

$$= \frac{1,248 - (4,620 \times 0.2612)}{12}$$

$$= \frac{1,248 - 1,206.74}{12}$$

$$= 3.438$$

The *a* coefficient is the fixed monthly expense. When *a* and *b* are taken together, they show that estimated monthly expenses equal a fixed component (*a*) of 3.438, plus an incremental cost (*b*) of .2612 per hour billed.

We will assume that your budget for the coming year will be based on a forecast of hours billed at four levels: 350, 375, 400, and 425 hours. The purpose of the regression line formula is to find the dependent variable *Y*. Estimates of future hours take on the value *X*. And we now have values for coefficients *a* and *b*. The formula is:

$$Y = a + bX$$

When we substitute the forecast estimates in the formula, remembering that we have summarized monthly expenses in hundreds of dollars, we get the following amounts:

350 hours
$$Y = 3.438 + (.2612 \times 350)$$
$$= 94.86 \ (\$9,486)$$

375 hours
$$Y = 3.438 + (.2612 \times 375)$$
$$= 101.39 \ (\$10,139)$$

400 hours
$$Y = 3.438 + (.2612 \times 400)$$
$$= 107.92 \ (\$10,792)$$

425 hours
$$Y = 3.438 + (.2612 \times 425)$$
$$= 114.45 \ (\$11,445)$$

This information can now be entered on a diagram, as shown in Figure 7-4. The estimated monthly expenses are listed in hundreds from top to bottom, and the number of assumed hours to be billed runs from left to right. Each of the computed value intersects is represented by dots:

Figure 7-4.   Regressive expense estimate.

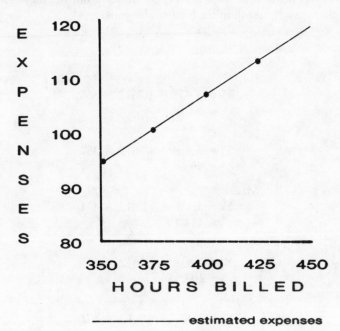

(hundreds)

estimated expenses

Expenses	Hours
94.86	350
101.39	375
107.92	400
114.45	425

DEPENDABILITY OF ESTIMATES

The regression line is an estimate of future expense levels, assuming a relationship between expenses and hours billed. You can also judge the dependability of estimates by taking the computation a step further. To begin, it's first necessary to estimate the value of Y from the historical information being used. You do this by working out the regression line formula for each month in the historical summary:

Jan
$$Y = 3.438 + (.2612 \times 365)$$
$$= 98.78$$

Feb
$$Y = 3.438 + (.2612 \times 357)$$
$$= 96.69$$

Mar
$$Y = 3.438 + (.2612 \times 424)$$
$$= 114.19$$

Apr
$$Y = 3.438 + (.2612 \times 381)$$
$$= 102.95$$

May
$$Y = 3.438 + (.2612 \times 362)$$
$$= 97.99$$

Jun
$$Y = 3.438 + (.2612 \times 405)$$
$$= 109.22$$

Jul
$$Y = 3.438 + (.2612 \times 406)$$
$$= 109.48$$

Aug
$$Y = 3.438 + (.2612 \times 392)$$
$$= 105.83$$

Sep
$$Y = 3.438 + (.2612 \times 365)$$
$$= 98.78$$

$$Oct$$
$$Y = 3.438 + (.2612 \times 417)$$
$$= 112.36$$

$$Nov$$
$$Y = 3.438 + (.2612 \times 394)$$
$$= 106.35$$

$$Dec$$
$$Y = 3.438 + (.2612 \times 352)$$
$$= 95.38$$

Next, build a table to compute the amount of deviation between the estimated values of Y (above) and actual historical values. The deviations, when squared can be used to judge the dependability of the regression analysis.

Table 2 consists of estimated Y (the values computed above), actual Y (historical information), the deviation (Y less estimated Y), and the square of the deviation:

Table 2. Measuring deviation.

Month	Estimated Y	Y	Deviation	Deviation²
Jan	$ 98.78	$ 96	−2.78	7.73
Feb	96.69	94	−2.69	7.24
Mar	114.19	111	−3.19	10.18
Apr	102.95	105	2.05	4.20
May	97.99	95	−2.99	8.94
Jun	109.22	110	0.78	0.61
Jul	109.48	109	−0.48	0.23
Aug	105.83	111	5.17	26.73
Sep	98.78	100	1.22	1.49
Oct	112.36	112	−0.36	0.13
Nov	106.35	107	0.65	0.42
Dec	95.38	98	2.62	6.86
Total	$1,248.00	$1,248	0.00	74.76

Note that estimated Y and acutual historical Y have identical totals. Estimated Y is nothing more than a rearrangement of the monthly totals based on the regression line formula you worked out previously. The purpose of this comparison is to determine the deviation from average. Deviation always totals zero, because the actual and estimated involve the same totals. The deviations, when squared, provide a means for calculating degree of error in the regression line. You can perform additional computations with the information developed to this point that will enable you to define your regression line in terms of relative predictability.

ESTIMATING ACCURACY

When you attend a budget meeting and present a neat, simple regression diagram for your estimate of the coming year, you will have to expect questions: How did you come up with this estimate? Where are the supporting data and assumptions? How *accurate* is this diagram?

To answer these questions, you may need to be able to explain the degree of deviation. Three formulas can be used to achieve this, each of which indicates how accurate your predictions are in comparison with other regression diagrams. You may not want to take the time to explain the statistical techniques you used, but you will be able to attach a percentage of dependability to the numbers you produce.

The first calculation is called the **standard error of estimate.** This is a very precise measurement of the deviation range you may expect to encounter in a particular regression line.

To compute it, you first need to figure out the **degrees of freedom** involved in your calculation. This represents the number of test areas or

----

standard error of estimate—a precise measurement of the range of deviation to be expected in a regression analysis. It is computed by finding the square root of the sum of deviations squared, then dividing by the degrees of freedom.

degrees of freedom—the number of values or quantities tested in statistics.

----

periods, less the number of coefficients involved. In our example, we based our regression line on 12 test periods (months). And because we have two coefficients (a and b), the degrees of freedom are 10:

Number of periods tested	12
Less coefficients	– 2
Degrees of freedom	10

The standard error of estimate formula is shown in Figure 7-5. In our example, deviation squared totals 74.76. This amount comes from Table 2 and is the total of the column "Deviation². " We first divide this by the degrees of freedom:

$$74.76 / 10 = 7.476$$

The square root of this amount is 2.73, the standard error of estimate. It tells you that in two-thirds of all instances, an estimate of the value of Y will not deviate from actual Y by more than 2.73; and that in one-third of all instances, you should expect an estimate to deviate by more than 2.73.

You can test this assumption by looking at the amount of deviation in Table 2. In the column "Deviation," we find that the four distances are more than 2.73:

Figure 7-5.   Standard error of estimate.

$$e = \sqrt{d^2 / f}$$

e = standard error of estimate
d^2 = deviation squared
f = degree of freedom

Jan	2.78
Mar	3.19
May	2.99
Aug	5.17

That's 4 out of 12, or one-third of the total number of deviations. The other 8 months, or two-thirds, reflect deviations lower than 2.73.

From this test, you can establish that your regression line conforms to the standard error of estimate. In one respect, this is a test of accuracy of the calculations involved; in another sense, it confirms that your regression line shows a reasonable estimate of the future relationship between a and b coefficients.

ESTIMATING DEPENDABILITY

Testing the accuracy of an assumption is only one of the two steps involved in validating the regression line. Next you want to ask, How dependable is the projection of the future?

Dependability is tested with the **coefficient of determination**, a test of sample variation.

----

coefficient of determination—a ratio of total sample variation, represented by the symbol R^2.

The formula for coefficient of determination is shown in Figure 7-6. The computation involves a division of deviation squared (this is the total of the column "Deviation²" in Table 2, or 74.76) by the total of y^2 (this total, 530, comes from Table 1). The result of this division is subtracted from 1:

$$R^2 = 1 - \left(\frac{74.76}{530}\right)$$

$$= 1 - .14106$$

$$= 0.85894$$

As a measure of dependability, the coefficient of determination formula reveals that on a scale of between -1 and $+1$, your estimate of future value is 0.85894. A -1 result is considered the least reliable, and a $+1$ is the most reliable or precise. So a 0.85894 result is fairly high on the scale.

Figure 7-6.   Coefficient of determination.

$$R^2 = 1 - \left(\frac{d^2}{Y^2} \right)$$

R^2 = coefficient of determination
d^2 = deviation squared
Y^2 = deviation from the mean of Y squared

Determination of dependability can be taken one additional step. The **coefficient of correlation** is a formula that summarizes the correlation between two variables. In our example, we use variables of hours billed and monthly expenses. How closely correlated are these data according to the least-squares exercise and regression line you have developed?

----

coefficient of correlation—a measurement of the correlation between two samples or between two variables.

The formula for coefficient of correlation is shown in Figure 7-7. The coefficient is represented by the symbol R, and the formula involves finding the square root of R^2 (coefficient of determination). In our example, this is $.85894$, and the square root of that total is $.92679$.

Figure 7-7.   Coefficient of correlation.

$$R = \sqrt{R^2}$$

R = coefficient of correlation
R² = coefficient of determination

This calculation reveals that, based on the regression analysis, the correlation is .92679 on a scale between zero (no correlation whatsoever) and 1 (a perfect correlation).

THE CAUTIOUS APPROACH

Regression analysis is based on the assumption that the relationship between variables is dependable. In practice, taking one variable to higher or lower levels could distort the assumed relationship so that your analysis would not be accurate. A straight line like the one you develop on a regression diagram may apply for only a limited range of the relationship.

Example: The comparison between hours billed and average monthly expenses is valid for a specific range of activity. After a certain amount of volume has been attained, however, expense levels tend to flatten out.

Outside circumstances may also distort the predictability of your regression line. This could add another dimension to your analysis, requiring that estimates be adjusted even further.

Example: You may project a significant increase in hours billed; however, there is a regional limit in the demand for the type of consultation services your firm offers.

You may face one of several circumstances that will affect the validity of your assumptions:

1. *The value of one variable is directly influenced by changes in another variable.* This is the assumption used in this chapter to describe regression line analysis. As long as the assumption concerning the relationship is valid, the regression line is applicable.

2. *The relationship has limitations.* Your variables may be closely related, but only to a degree. The range you explore (for example, using historical information) may not reflect the limitation. It could be that the variability of expenses will be different when hours billed exceed 400 per month, for example.

3. *A third variable affects the two you test.* There is also the possibility that your two variables are not truly related, but move in a similar manner owing to the influence of a third variable. For example, it could be that expense controls are relaxed in proportion to the level of hours billed; or when more people are on the payroll, total hours and monthly expenses are both affected. In this case, the comparison and study of hours and expenses may not be a valid test to perform. For this reason, it is essential that you understand the attributes of the variables and that you are certain that they interact in the way assumed.

4. The relationship is coincidental. The similar changes in hours billed and expense levels could be a matter of chance occurrence. Although this may seem unlikely, it is possible. You can test a larger sample to eliminate this possibility.

Any statistical study can be only as accurate as the underlying assumptions. Once you know that the information used is applicable and accurate, you may proceed with confidence. But even then, estimates should be tested, and tests should be given limits. Chapter 8 explains how to manage data and estimate outcomes with limitations in mind.

WORK PROJECT

1. Your company is considering changing banks. You have the task of estimating bank charges on the basis of varying numbers of checks

written each month. One institution charges a monthly fee of $8 plus 15¢ for each check cleared during the month.

Compute the amount of charge each month using the regression line formula:

$$Y = a + bX$$

Use the following figures for the number of checks written each month:

a. 150 checks
b. 225 checks
c. 300 checks

2. Over the last six months, your company had varying numbers of employees on the payroll and experienced varying levels of selling expenses. Totals are:

Month	Employees	Expenses ($ 00)
Jan	42	$129
Feb	43	130
Mar	41	126
Apr	46	132
May	44	130
Jun	48	133
Total	264	$780
Mean	44	$130

a. Complete calculations for the least-squares analysis using the table below. Assume that X = employees and that Y = expenses per month (in hundreds).

Month	X	Y	x	y	x^2	y^2	xy
Jan	___	$___	___	___	___	___	___
Feb	___	___	___	___	___	___	___
Mar	___	___	___	___	___	___	___
Apr	___	___	___	___	___	___	___
May	___	___	___	___	___	___	___
Jun	___	___	___	___	___	___	___
Total	___	$___	___	___	___	___	___
Mean	___	$___					

b. Compute the values of coefficients b and a using the formulas:

$$b = \frac{xy}{x^2} \qquad a = \frac{Y - (Xb)}{n}$$

3. Using the same information in question 2, compute the future levels of selling expenses, assuming payroll grows to the following levels:
   a. 50 employees
   b. 55 employees
   c. 60 employees

8

Estimating With Confidence

Facts are seldom facts, but what people think are facts, tinged with assumptions.

—Harold Geneen

"I just finished up in the budget review meeting," an exhausted manager told a friend. "It was tough. We were way off on our projections, and I had to explain why."

"How did you do?" the friend asked.

"At first, I tried to tell them we simply made a mistake, but they wouldn't accept that explanation. So then I said that our hypothesis had not included the entire scope of probabilities, and the outcome fell outside of the range we had used."

"And?"

"They loved it."

You're unable to sleep. You pace a lot. You've never been the type to take your work-related problems home, but now you can't get work out of your mind. All because you're not happy about having to put yourself on the line with an *estimate* instead of something more absolute.

As troubling as it is, we have to estimate the future because we don't always have enough facts to pin down the future in absolute terms or because historical information just isn't enough to guide us. But some statistical techniques can help you to overcome these problems.

In previous chapters, you saw how probabilities can be narrowed down or defined when a range of possible outcomes is well understood. For example, correctly judging the likelihood of success has a 50-50 chance; but you may need to estimate degrees of success or failure: How much will you be likely to gain or lose? Now consider the other side of the question: How do you test an assumption and draw conclusions about it? How do you interpret sample results to estimate what they tell you about the future, or how accurately sample results indicate the likely outcome of a population?

THE PURPOSE OF ESTIMATING

You will be expected to estimate a wide range of future outcomes in the course of your job. You can use past experiences to support a point of view or to suggest a decision, or you can develop statistically based methods for interpreting what past samples reveal. Estimating is necessary in many business applications, including:

■ *Assessing risks*. Your approach to a problem should always be undertaken with risk in mind. The executive who must decide to approve or disapprove an action is constantly aware of the risks. Present information that addresses that concern.

Example: Your company is thinking about expanding its market territory. During a meeting, you and other managers have been asked to offer opinions. Based on previous expansion, sample testing, and market demand, what are the risks? How can the company commit the least amount of investment capital to gain the most information about future profits?

■ *Setting standards*. You also estimate to set operational standards for the future. The budget is one example of this. With a budget, you have a standard against which actual results will be judged. The budgeting process should not be thought of as a means for guessing actual results; instead, it sets up a reasonable expectation of outcome. Then, when actual results vary, you can examine the causes and try to improve the process the next time around, as well as identify areas where more control is needed.

Example: While investigating a significant expense variance, you discover that spending procedures are poorly controlled. As a result, you recommend a change that will reduce future expense levels.

■ *Feasibility judgment.* Estimates help compare risk and reward. It's not enough just to identify future cost and expense levels or likely volume of sales, or to suggest an internal change just because it's desirable. The real bottom line is: What are the risks in comparison with the potential rewards?

Example: You are recommending to management that the recurring procedures in your department be automated. Your study compares today's processing costs with assumed savings through automation. On a manual basis, you will have to hire additional employees in coming years just to handle volume. One approach is to complain about the amount of work you have and warn that additional volume will mean even more work. Another approach is to compare risk (the cost of buying automated systems and training employees) with potential reward (savings in future payroll costs). Is the idea feasible? And how long will it take the company to recapture its investment?

■ *Support for ideas.* Closely related to feasibility is the idea of supporting recommendations. An idea may be considered feasible but not necessary. In this case, an estimate of future profits or other benefits may make a difference in the decision.

Example: You want to relocate your department to the third floor. One benefit would be that you'd gain more space, which you'll need to house the employees you plan to hire during the coming year. You also point out to management that most of the contact in your department takes place on the third floor, and being there would increase efficiency. That increased efficiency can be estimated in terms of future savings to support your recommendation.

■ *Response to requests.* When you are asked to provide information, it's rare that the other person only wants a summary of the past. It's more likely that the reason for making the request is to estimate the future.

Example: During a management meeting, a discussion concerning customer complaints leads the president to ask you for a summary of recent trends. Anticipating the president's interest, you don't limit your report to a passive summary of complaint trends; you also estimate what the trends mean, and where you expect them to lead.

HYPOTHESIS TESTING

The disturbing fact about estimates is that you don't always know whether your underlying assumptions are correct. Even when a problem is specifically understood, you may not have the facts available to make the estimate. The more uncertain you are about your assumptions, the less comfortable you will be with your estimate.

A **hypothesis** (unproved theory) contains an assumption or a series of assumptions. In order to proceed with confidence in making an estimate, you must validate and prove that your assumptions are sound. To test a hypothesis, you need to examine the statistical information used to make your estimate, or analyze the results of sample data to judge likely future events on a larger scale. The purpose of the test is to prove or disprove the hypothesis.

----

hypothesis testing—the examination of a body of evidence or statistical results to determine whether to accept or reject the underlying assumptions.

It's a mistake to look only for confirming information. That process assumes that the hypothesis is correct and leads to selection of one series of facts and rejection of all others. A valid hypothesis test is objective. It is undertaken to prove or disprove, on the premise that a valid hypothesis leads to accurate estimates. On the other hand, a disproved hypothesis shows that an alternative should be developed before proceeding.

Example: Your company is introducing a new product to the market. No similar products have been tested in the past, and the potential buyer is a new customer. You have no historical information on which to base your estimate, so you will need to analyze the results of limited samples from tests. Those tests may provide dependable information if the hypothesis behind the testing method is correct; or they may mislead if the test is not fair and does not represent the responses of a larger population.

Example: You recommend a major change in procedures on the premise that it will reduce expenses. However, you have no specific past information to support this belief and will have to operate on a series of assumptions. If the assumptions do relate to issues that will reduce future expenses, then the hypothesis is valid.

Example: You are working on a budget for a newly formed department. All expenses will have to be estimated without historical information or trends. If your base of assumptions is reasonable, then the estimates expressed in the budget are fair as well; but if the historical information you use does not apply to the new department, there's no reason to expect the budget to represent a fair estimate.

In each case, you will need to develop estimates based on a hypothesis. A new product stands the risk of not being accepted by the market. A change in procedures could cost a lot of money and produce no measurable results. And the budget for a new department cannot be supported from past experience. You can solve these problems by conducting limited tests.

Example: The new product is tested in one or two markets for a limited period of time. The results are used to judge the likely degree of market acceptance on a much larger scale, in the belief that the preferences of consumers in the test market fairly represent a larger population.

Example: The time required to complete a limited number of tasks is evaluated and summarized. An alternative is then presented, with estimates of the differences in cost. This test is then applied on a larger scale and the total savings estimated. From this, you can indicate the time required to recapture the cost of the change.

Example: Your budget for a new department is built on assumptions from experience in other departments. Office supply, telephone, and transportation expenses are estimated on a per-employee basis; rent, insurance, and maintenance expenses are budgeted on a percentage of square feet the department will occupy. Although you are still limited to estimation, the basis of assumption is reasonable.

A lot of energy is put into developing elaborate estimates of future outcomes without first establishing a dependable series of assumptions. Budgeting may be such an example in your company. How much effort is put into the development of assumptions, testing those assumptions, and tracking results? In some cases, energy goes not into a logical approach to the question but into figuring out how to explain away the outcomes that don't agree. The entire budgeting process may begin not with a valid hypothesis but with a predetermined conclusion. The budget is then manipulated until it reaches the conclusion you want. That's a misuse of estimation.

Remember the purpose of an estimate: to develop a reasonable or likely outcome or range of outcomes, not to merely guess the "right" answer. Even though this is logical and obvious, it's easily overlooked when you're up to your elbows in worksheets and putting in ten-hour days in budget review meetings.

MEASURING OUTCOMES

You have gathered information and want to measure results so that your estimate of the future will be reasonable. But the problem is, you're not sure how to make your measurement. How do you define a significant variation from expected to actual results in a sample? This problem applies to many situations involving estimates.

Example: You're working on a budget revision at the end of six months. Some accounts show unfavorable variance results. How should the revised budget be altered?

Example: A market test of product preferences produces somewhat different results between regions. Is the variation the result of random chance, or does it indicate a difference worth investigating?

Example: The marketing department has summarized recent activity for several salespeople. Varying numbers met assigned quotas in each division. Does this mean that some divisions are better supervised or contain a higher caliber of salespeople? Or are the different degrees within what you should consider an "acceptable" range?

A measurement called **chi-square** can help you to decide degrees of significance in variances, especially when comparative tests or samples are used for the estimate. Chi-square is notated as X^2.

----

chi-square—a measurement of differences in outcomes of tests, used to identify degrees of significance.

The hypothesis at work in a chi-square test is that two variables are independent. Chi-square proves or disproves that hypothesis. By examining the degree of difference and comparing it to the expected degree, you can conclude that (1) the difference is *not* significant or (2) the difference is significant, meaning that the expected value criteria are flawed.

Example: You work for a life insurance company. Management expects consumers in different regions to have similar preference levels for two different products you offer—whole life and term insurance. However, the results of a survey show that the expected levels of preference are not the same. By applying the chi-square test, you can compare the survey results to the results you assumed to be within an acceptable range.

The marketing vice-president has summarized the previous year's sales by the number of consumers who responded positively to each product:

| Product | Number of Positive Responses | | |
	Region A	Region B	Total
Whole life	462	504	966
Term	536	452	988
Total	998	956	1,954

The question in this example is, Are the reported differences significant, and if so, to what degree? To answer, you first need to define your null hypothesis (the assumption for your study) and then identify the expectation for outcome.

COMPARING THE HYPOTHESIS

The null hypothesis is: PREFERENCES IN DIFFERENT REGIONS WILL CONFORM TO OVERALL RESULTS. Collectively, 966 people responded positively to the whole life product. That represents 49.4 percent of the total positive responses to either product. And 988 responded positively to term insurance; that's 50.6 percent.

The expectation is that these overall positive responses will apply in each region. If that is true, the following results would have been observed:

Region A, whole life: 49.4% of 998, or 493
Region B, whole life: 49.4% of 956, or 472
Region A, term: 50.6% of 998, or 505
Region B, term: 50.6% of 956, or 484

The chi-square test is performed by squaring the differences between expected and actual outcomes. The squared differences are then divided by expected outcome:

Expected Outcome	Actual Outcome	Difference	Difference²	Chi-Square
493	462	31	961	1.95
472	504	−32	1,024	2.17
505	536	−31	961	1.90
484	452	32	1,024	2.12
				8.14

The third column is the result of subtracting column 2 from column 1. The first line, for example, gives:

$$493 - 462 = 31$$

Note that the differences offset so that the sum is always zero. That's because the total of the tests is the same. Expected and actual outcomes deal with the same total count, but they're rearranged.

The last column is the result of dividing the squared differences by the first column, expected outcome:

$$\frac{961}{493} = 1.95$$

$$\frac{1,024}{472} = 2.17$$

$$\frac{961}{505} = 1.90$$

$$\frac{1,024}{484} = 2.12$$

The calculation can also be expressed as a formula, which is shown in Figure 8-1. This formula states: CHI-SQUARE EQUALS THE SUM OF EXPECTED VALUES LESS ACTUAL VALUES, SQUARED; DIVIDED BY EXPECTED VALUE.

Figure 8-1. Chi-square.

$$x^2 = \frac{(E-A)^2}{E}$$

x^2 = chi-square
E = expected outcome
A = actual outcome

Substituting the values from the chi-square table above in the formula (Figure 8-1), we have:

$$\frac{(493-462)^2}{493} + \frac{(472-504)^2}{472} + \frac{(505-536)^2}{505} + \frac{(484-452)^2}{484} = 8.14$$

Now you know that the chi square of your problem is 8.14. But what does that mean in terms of significance and whether or not your assumption is correct? To learn this, we must identify the degrees of freedom at work. You will recall that *degrees of freedom* are the number of test areas or quantities in which a statistical trial is conducted.

In our example, product preferences are tested in two regions, meaning there are two degrees of freedom in the test. With that in mind, you next have to decide what consitutes a significant degree of variance in test results. For example, you may decide to evaluate your test on the assumption that it is acceptable for regional differences to vary as often as 5 percent of the time. Thus, you will want to compare the chi-square result of 8.14 with a table of chi-square distributions. These table values require a computer to calculate, but published tables are available. Table 3 shows chi-square distributions at several levels and for several degrees of freedom.

Table 3. Variation testing.

Degrees of Freedom	Significance Level				
	.01	.05	.10	.25	.50
2	9.2	6.0	4.6	2.8	1.4
3	11.3	7.8	6.2	4.1	2.4
4	13.3	9.5	7.8	5.4	3.4
5	15.1	11.1	9.2	6.6	4.4
6	16.8	12.6	10.6	7.8	5.3
7	18.5	14.1	12.0	9.0	6.4
8	20.1	15.5	13.4	10.2	7.3
9	21.7	16.9	14.7	11.4	8.3
10	23.2	18.3	15.9	12.5	9.3
11	24.7	19.7	17.3	13.7	10.3
12	26.2	21.0	18.6	14.8	11.3
13	27.7	22.4	19.8	16.0	12.3
14	29.1	23.7	21.1	17.1	13.3
15	30.6	25.0	22.3	18.2	14.3
16	32.0	26.3	23.5	19.4	15.3
17	33.4	27.6	24.8	20.5	16.3
18	34.8	28.9	26.0	21.6	17.3
19	36.2	30.1	27.2	22.7	18.3
20	37.6	31.4	28.4	23.8	19.3

We assumed that .05 was the acceptable range of variation—meaning a specified level of variation will be expected 5 percent of the time—and that in 95 percent of cases, variation should be lower than the chi-square value. The 8.14 chi-square result should be judged using the .05 column. For two degrees of freedom, the table shows that the expected maximum chi-square is 6.0. This tells you that chi-square should be less than 6.0 in 95 percent of cases (.05 subtracted from 1). The actual chi-square of 8.14 is significant, based on this test. Therefore, the null hypothesis—that preferences in different regions for the two types of insurance will conform to overall results—should be rejected.

EXPANDING THE TEST

The same test can be applied to problems encompassing a larger scope of analysis. Chi-square can help identify the significance of variance for a number of comparative samples.

Example: The marketing vice-president presents you with a summary of recent sales activity in eight regions. The concern is with trying to figure out why results are not consistent among different regions. But the real question is, "Do the results reflect a significant degree of difference, or are the results within an acceptable range?" The summary shows the number of salespeople who met their quotas. You and the vice-president agree that based on that summary, variance should occur in no more than 10 percent of all cases. That is not an exact estimate of how much variance you may expect. Choosing 10 percent, rather than 5 or 20 or 30 percent, is a matter of judgment. But when consistent definitions of "significance" are applied to similar situations, a relative conclusion can be reached. For example, the test of sales quota results could be applied on a quarterly basis to decide whether or not variations in several divisions are acceptable.

The information you receive from the marketing vice-president shows:

Region	Number of People	Reaching Quota Number	Reaching Quota Percentage
A	114	89	78.1%
B	93	76	81.7
C	106	84	79.2
D	123	98	79.7
E	84	69	82.1
F	101	77	76.2
G	96	79	82.3
H	107	82	76.6
Overall	824	654	79.4%

The question is, Is the variance between each region and the overall percentage a significant one?

To come up with an answer, first break out the eight regions into two expectation groups based on the overall outcome, one group representing the 79.4 percent of all people expected to meet quota, the other group representing the 20.6 percent of people expected not to meet the quota. Next, compare expected outcome to actual outcome to develop chi-square. In this example, there are eight degrees of freedom (one for each region). For the sake of distinction, we will designate the 79.4 percent group + and the 20.6 percent group −, meaning Region A is broken into A + and A −, Region B into B + and B −, and so forth.

After expected outcomes are listed, actual results are posted. We have assumed that you expect a variance to occur 10 percent of the time. This means the .10 chi-square distribution table should be used to test these variances. The worksheet looks like this:

Region	Number of People		Diff.	Diff.^{2}	Chi Square
	Expected Outcome	Actual Outcome			
A +	91	89	2	4	0.04
A −	23	25	−2	4	0.17
B +	74	76	−2	4	0.05
B −	19	17	2	4	0.21
C +	84	84	0	0	0.00
C −	22	22	0	0	0.00
D +	98	98	0	0	0.00
D −	25	25	0	0	0.00
E +	67	69	−2	4	0.06
E −	17	15	2	4	0.24
F +	80	77	3	9	0.11
F −	21	24	−3	9	0.43
G +	76	79	−3	9	0.12
G −	20	17	3	9	0.45
H +	85	82	3	9	0.11
H −	22	25	−3	9	0.41
	824	824			2.40

Referring to the chi-square distribution table (Table 3) and the column for .10 (the assumed level of variation), you will see that expectation for eight degrees of freedom (one per region) is 13.4. This means that there is a 90 percent chance that variances will be lower than a chi-square of 13.4. Your chi-square was calculated at 2.40, meaning the variance is not significant. Thus you may conclude that the outcomes prove that expectations were reasonable.

MEASURING SAMPLE DEVIATION

You may face a different problem when trying to interpret the results of a sample. How can you establish whether or not a variation is significant based on the outcome of a test? What degree of deviation is to be expected? While chi-square tests outcomes compared to a preconceived standard, sample deviation tests outcomes to decide a degree of significance in variation.

Example: Your company is preparing to put a new product on the market. Your research department devised a test to see how consumers would respond to different packaging. Some products were offered in a blue box and others in a yellow box. In the first test, 100 people were asked to choose between the blue-boxed new product and a well-established competing brand. In the second test, 100 people were asked to choose between the yellow-boxed new product and the same competing brand. The results were:

- 22 percent chose the blue box over the competing brand.
- 29 percent chose the yellow box over the competing brand.

On the basis of this result, some managers and executives believe the test proves consumers respond to the yellow box better than to the blue box. Others believe the difference doesn't prove anything. How can the results be more specifically judged?

A calculation called the **standard error of difference** can provide you with a measurement of sample results. With this formula, you can estimate how much deviation should be expected.

----

standard error of difference—a measurement of the percentage by which a sample is likely to deviate from the average.

The formula for standard error of difference is shown in Figure 8-2. Applying this formula to our example, we have:

$$S = \sqrt{\frac{22\ (100-22)}{200} + \frac{29\ (100-29)}{200}}$$

$$= \sqrt{\frac{22 \times 78}{200} + \frac{20 \times 71}{200}}$$

$$= \sqrt{8.58 + 10.295}$$

$$= 4.34$$

You would expect a deviation of 4.34 percent. Actual outcome of the sample reflected a 7 percent difference, which should be considered

Figure 8-2. Standard error of difference.

$$S = \sqrt{\frac{A\ (100-A)}{n} + \frac{B\ (100-B)}{n}}$$

S = standard error of difference
A = percentage of outcome **A**
B = percentage of outcome **B**
n = number of total tests

significant. This indicates that the yellow box is better received than the blue box.

All of the statistical tests you apply will be only as accurate as the information you receive and will give conclusions that are only as good as your hypothesis. The most troublesome aspect of estimating is that without first testing and validating information, you can never be sure that your conclusion is reasonable. You can never be absolutely sure about an estimate; but you can gain a degree of comfort by first testing the validity of information you use in your test. You'll see how validating information is the subject to Chapter 9.

WORK PROJECT

1. Your company recently test-marketed two products in two regions. People were asked to choose between product 1 and product 2. The results were:

	Number of Total Responses		
	Region A	*Region B*	*Total*
Product 1	241	256	497
Product 2	279	214	493
Total	520	470	990

a. Explain the null hypothesis from overall results.
b. List expectation results for:

Region A, product 1 _____

Region B, product 1 _____

Region A, product 2 _____

Region B, product 2 _____

c. Use the worksheet below to compute chi-square:

Expected Outcome	Actual Outcome	Difference	Difference²	Chi-Square
_____	_____	_____	_____	_____
_____	_____	_____	_____	_____
_____	_____	_____	_____	_____
_____	_____	_____	_____	_____

d. Show the same calculation using the formula for chi-square given in this chapter.

2. Using the same data in question 1, answer the following:
   a. How many degrees of freedom are involved?
   b. If you assume that variances are expected to occur in 10 percent of cases, what is the maximum chi-square distribution? (Use the table given in this chapter.)
   c. Is the variance significant? Why or why not?

3. Your company is considering offering extended warranty contracts on certain products it sells. A recent survey of 200 customers in two regions asked the question, "Would you be inclined to buy an extended warranty contract for $35 on items that cost more than $500?" Here are the results:

Region	Positive Responses
A	31%
B	35%

a. Compute the standard error of difference using the formula given in this chapter.
b. Is the deviation significant? Why or why not?

9

Proving That the Numbers Work

Great blunders are often made, like large ropes, of a multitude of fibers.

—Victor Hugo

The accounting department was working on a marketing plan for the coming year, with most of the risk evaluation work done by two employees. During a break, the subject of American history came up.

"I never realized before how close we came to losing the Revolutionary War," one commented to the other.

"What do you mean?"

"Well, they didn't understand the risks," the first one explained. "If they'd had the budget to hire a statistician, they never would have declared independence."

A pool player shooting down the length of the table is off by a hair, and the ball misses the pocket. The same type of minor miscalculation can affect the accuracy of your business forecasts. It's not the same as shooting pool, but the result is the same. You'll miss if you don't measure correctly.

It's not just a single mistake that leads to wrong conclusions or to projections way off the mark. As often as not, a series of errors add up to a bigger problem. Mistakes can occur in:

1. *The numbers.* If your projections are based on the wrong use of numbers, or on numbers that don't even add up correctly, your estimated outcome will be off.

Example: You are a marketing manager preparing a summary of sales volume produced by the average salesperson during the previous year. The purpose is to give newly hired employees a goal. But the numbers used were for all salespeople, including those with years of experience and a well-established contact network. Your estimated quota level is too high.

Example: You are working on a budget and base the estimated expense levels on the monthly averages of the previous year. But you forgot to check the math, and the 12 months' totals are off by several thousand dollars.

2. *The raw data.* Information used to prepare estimates or to evaluate risks should be directly related and valid; otherwise, your results will have no meaning.

Example: You are attempting to estimate the time required to complete a task in your department. But the sample task you use in your test is completely different from the task under study. As a consequence, your estimate of time required is way off.

Example: You are working on a report suggesting that expenses will be reduced if the company invests in new equipment. You ask the accounting department for a summary of maintenance expenses. They misunderstand your request and send the wrong list.

3. *Assumptions.* A conclusion reached will be only as dependable as the hypothesis on which it's based. If your assumption has not been tested and validated, you are not ready to proceed.

Example: Several accounts in this year's budget were estimated on the basis of what the marketing department said they would generate in sales. But after you prepared your budget, sales forecast totals were revised. Your variable expense budgets are based on invalid assumptions.

Example: Your company performs a test for a new product in a single market. The assumption is that the region selected is representative of the entire country. Results are much lower than you expected. Upon looking at the region more closely, you discover that most of the jobs in the area are with one company, and they laid off hundreds of people less than a month before your test.

PUTTING INFORMATION TO USE

Try this experiment: Give two people in your department identical information and then ask them to prepare reports that draw conclusions. You will discover that two people will come back with different answers in a large number of cases.

Example: You are the manager of a customer service department. During the last six months, the following number of complaint calls and letters were received:

Jan	43
Feb	48
Mar	55
Apr	43
May	69
Jun	81

You ask two employees in your department to prepare brief reports explaining this trend and its significance. One employee turns in a report that compares the number of complaint calls per employee in the department:

	Calls	*Staff*	*Ratio*
Jan	43	7	6.1
Feb	48	7	6.9
Mar	55	7	7.9
Apr	54	7	7.7
May	69	8	8.6
Jun	81	8	10.1

This employee's report concludes that the average employee in the department is handling many more calls and letters now than six months ago. The report observes that a further increase could reduce response time and quality.

The second employee's report compares the rate of increase in complaints to the rate of increase in sales volume:

	Calls	Percentage Increase	Sales ($000)	Percentage Increase
Jan	43	—	423.5	—
Feb	48	12%	481.0	14%
Mar	55	15	559.8	16
Apr	54	-2	563.3	1
May	69	28	729.1	29
Jun	81	17	882.0	21

This report points out that the rate of increase in complaints from customers is less than the rate of increase in sales; thus, the trend is not negative. The report also points out that the change in sales and in complaints reflects a seasonal trend that closely follows patterns seen in previous years. Sales volume has been growing steadily, the report states, and a corresponding change in complaints is to be expected.

Both reports make valid points and contain reasonable observations. Neither is wrong, but different sets of conclusions were reached because the raw data were subjected to different tests. In other words, the two employees assumed different questions in developing their answers.

The first report demonstrates that in the future it will be necessary to hire additional employees to handle the volume of complaints. Sales are on the increase, as confirmed by the second report; so the observation about future staffing needs is a valid one. This report was prepared from an internal point of view. The question asked was, "What does this increase mean to the department? What steps should be taken in response to the trend?"

The second report takes a different point of view. By comparing the rate of increase to sales, a more external point of view, the question being asked is, "Do these results reflect a positive or a negative trend?"

If each employee had been given clearer instructions in procedure, it's likely that their reports would have at least been based on the same information. For example, you might have given the instruction "Compare the increase in the rate of complaints to the increase in sales volume for the same period, and tell me whether this is a positive or a negative trend."

Even then, the conclusions reached by each employee might have been different. For example, using the same comparison (increase in complaints next to increase in sales), consider these conclusions:

Report A:

The rate of increase in customer complaints is lower than the corresponding increase in sales. This trend is positive, indicating that service and sales quality are being maintained at acceptable levels.

Report B:

Sales reflect a seasonal change, in line with similar volume patterns in past years. However, in the past, customer complaint trends did not vary to the degree seen in the past six months. This is a negative trend. The volume of complaints is following sales volume rather than remaining at more stable and predictable levels seen in the past.

Which conclusion is right? Should customer complaint levels be expected to remain stable, or should they vary with sales volume? That answer depends on the type of product or service you offer, the historical picture reviewed in total, and your own opinions as to valid assumptions.

The point here is that there is rarely one right answer, or one complete answer. Even a clearly communicated question can be interpreted differently. When you ask two employees to compare complaints with sales volume and comment on positive or negative trends, what does that mean? Are trends in the past positive or negative? Is your department more effective because of changed procedures and response techniques? Or are you less efficient as the result of ever-growing sales volume, changes in the field, or other influences?

TESTING VALIDITY

Before analyzing a set of raw data, you should make sure the question is well understood. This applies when you are executing a task, as well as when you give an assignment to someone else.

In the example of the customer complaint analysis, what question are you trying to answer? One possibility is, "Based on recent trends in customer complaints, is the trend positive or negative? The answer should be based on an evaluation of the current trend, in comparison with the same trend in the past."

The question has been qualified. The answer will depend on a number of considerations:

- Seasonal variation currently and in past years
- A comparison of results and variations
- Analysis of changes enacted during the year

For example, you may discover that sales are moving in the same pattern as in the past; however, customer complaint trends, which have not moved in the same direction as sales in the past, are doing so now. Why?

Before you can answer your first question, it may be necessary to find out what the change means. For example:

- Have you changed your response procedures? For example, are you doing a better job of tracking and recording complaints now? Do field offices convey or refer complaints differently from a year ago?
- Are customers better able to reach you or more aware of your service? Did you install a toll-free line, advertise your services, or undertake a survey?
- Have changes in the sales force or branch offices affected the trend? Are new salespeople being trained differently, or has sales leadership been changed? Are complaints coming more from one region than from others?

Getting the valid answer could demand a lot of secondary research in this case. As in many business problems, the question and the answer are not clear or simple. They're complex and involve many elements that affect outcome.

A dependable analysis is based on consistent testing of known quantities and comparisons. For example, if your company has tracked customer complaint trends for many years and compared them with sales activity, that's a good starting point. When you notice an unexpected change in the trend, it tells you that something has changed. Your job is to identify the cause or causes, and then to comment and make recommendations.

If you discover that complaints are rising in one region, it could indicate a leadership or training problem. If a change occurs after a major change in policy, promotion, or tracking, it could be a direct result of that change. Your report should emphasize three areas:

1. Significance of the change in a trend
2. Causes for the change
3. Recommendations to continue positive trends or reverse and correct negative trends

These areas are ones where statistical techniques presented in past chapters can help. Validity is best tested by applying the analytical tests of probability and outcome, to the likely changes that will occur in the future.

Example: You can evaluate customer complaints on the basis of the numbers, the percentage of increase from one month to another, or an index against an acceptable norm.

Example: Comparisons may be drawn with sales activity, between regions, or with changes in procedures, training, or personnel. Analysis may attempt to discover leveling-off points, if that applies, or anticipate how recent trends will affect the future.

APPLYING STATISTICAL TECHNIQUES

Your analysis of customer complaints could begin with a summary of the mean over a period of time longer than the most recent six months. You could calculate the mean on a moving average basis, or weight the most recent information. You could do the same with sales, then compare the relationship.

You can then compute the variance of the moving average with the mean absolute deviation method (see Chapter 2). Dispersion in each set could be calculated and compared over a period of time. From this series of tests, you could determine (a) whether or not the change is significant and the degree of significance on a percentage basis; (b) whether the situation has changed substantially from past years, perhaps when sales volume was lower; and (c) what corrective actions, if any, should be taken.

Another test you could use involves development of a graph showing the normal distribution of complaint frequency and a weighted average of modified expectation value in the future.

On the basis of assumptions about the probability of lower service quality with increased volume of sales, the formula for binomial distribution also could be applied to the problem to show how customer complaint activity varies with sales levels. And the comparison between complaints and sales would be an appropriate subject for regression analysis using the least-squares method—again, with assumptions based on past observations.

Further analysis of this type of problem will have practical applications if you survey customers. For example, you may ask for responses to changes in service policies. Samples can be evaluated and expected outcomes compared with actual outcomes by use of the chi-square method; and dependability of tests can be evaluated with the formula to measure the standard error of difference.

DRAWING CONCLUSIONS

In any application of statistical techniques, the real proof of value is in the results. If you develop risk analysis methods, probability studies, or sample evaluations a comparison to actual outcomes tells the real story.

Example: You spend a great deal of time and effort reducing your analysis of sample data to a few key conclusions. These are presented to management. When actual results come through, it turns out that your projections were exceptionally accurate. This validates your approach.

Example: You use statistical techniques to prepare your budget. But actual results show many significant variances, indicating that there is a problem. The flaw, however, is not with the techniques nor with their application. Rather, your underlying assumptions are not correct (or, in many cases, developments since the preparation of the budget has changed the operating environment, and the assumptions no longer apply).

There is great danger in confining your analysis to the past, to a selective field of raw data, or to information from only one source. The more raw data you gather and the more carefully you challenge your own hypothesis, the better your chances that outcomes can be predicted or that risks can be fairly evaluated. You may also have to modify an approach—even when it's worked in the past—because of recent changes in operation.

Example: In the past, your analysis of employee productivity was confined to a study of transactions processed. During the last year, though, the processing routines were automated, and your trend analysis is producing results that vary widely from expectation value. Because of automation, the environment has changed, and the old test no longer works.

Example: You prepare a report each month that compares actual sales production by representative with your original forecast. One division has been on the mark all year; but at the end of the year, it falls far below forecast. When you look into the situation, you discover that the sales manager has been providing production totals at the end of each month based not on the actual numbers, but on an overoptimistic estimate.

Example: When each regional sales manager supplies sales totals to you, that serves as one source of raw data. However, you also check with the accounting department to see what level of income has been booked. You know there's a delay in getting the final week's receipts to the bank and then onto the books; so you expect some variance. But what you're looking for is a major difference between each source. When one is discovered, you double-check with the sales manager to find out the reason.

You may end up picking your own facts selectively. This is a constant problem, especially when you begin with a hypothesis that you want to prove. A completely objective statistical analysis must include both the positive and the negative outcomes.

Example: You contend that purchasing an additional photocopy machine will be justified by savings in employee time. Currently, delays in work are caused by the fact that several departments use the only machine on your floor; and a growing frequency of maintenance problems adds to the expense.

You study maintenance costs for the past year and estimate the number of hours of delay your department experiences. Your intention is to prove that the company will recapture its investment in tangible savings within one year. You discover, however, that maintenance bills have not increased as substantially as you suspected; and the delays your employees experience are not as expensive as you believe at first.

You are tempted to estimate an increase in future maintenance costs and employee delays. However, the facts disprove your theory. A prudent alternative may be to not base the request on past history (because it disproves rather than supports your hypothesis); or to mention the lower-than-expected savings and extend your estimate of how long it will take the company to recapture its investment.

QUALIFYING RESULTS

Besides being as fair as possible in selecting raw data, also be careful about the way you express statistical conclusions. It's easy to distort the truth so that bad news sounds good or your hypothesis sounds right, even when the conclusion doesn't really support it.

Example: Your company participates in a softball league that was just started up, and ABC Company, your main competitor, is also in the league. An article in this month's company newsletter states, "Our team won second place this weekend. ABC came in second to last."

This is an example of how statistics can be distorted by the way they're selected. What the newsletter article failed to mention was that there are only two teams in the league. Thus, "second place" and "second to last" mean much different results.

The same distortion can be applied to the way business results are explained. In fact, annual reports that are sent to stockholders often make the worst of years sound the most promising.

Example: A company lost millions of dollars last year, for the third year in a row. The president's message to stockholders states:

> The slowdown in the rate of increase in year-to-year net losses is a promising trend, reflecting the results of constructive actions we've taken to achieve a profitable stance.

Example: A company reported a net loss last year due to a judgment in a major lawsuit. Before allowing for the loss, earnings were a record 9 percent return on sales. The emphasis in the annual report is on the record rather than on the bottom line:

> We are proud to report a record return on sales last year, before adjusting for a one-time extraordinary item. We expect this positive trend to sustain into the current year.

In both cases, the bad news is ignored or passed over, or at least expressed in positive terms. If they don't look at the financial statements, readers may conclude that their investment in company stock is quite safe and that management is taking good care of their money and making it grow.

You have probably seen the same cloaking of facts in explanations of budget variances:

The unfavorable variance of 19 percent reflects a slowdown in the negative trend, and indicates that by year-end, the variance rate will have stopped.

Payroll cost exceeds budget; however, no additional increase in the trend is expected for the balance of the year.

Profits are lower than expectations for the year-to-date due to unexpected seasonal slowdowns in volume.

None of these explanations identify the causes of variance, nor do they answer the question, "What can we do to reverse the negative trend?" That should be the purpose of going through the analysis; yet, the expression of statistical results hides the facts rather than reveals them.

Set these standards for reporting statistically:

1. *Express the outcome clearly.* There is a tendency to strongly proclaim good news but to talk around the bad. No matter what the outcome, clearly identify the problem and its scope, the cause, and the solution.

2. *Avoid manipulaiton.* Don't seek facts and figures that support the outcome you'd like to report. If the news is negative, your task should be to bring it to management's attention so that decisions can be made for corrective action. If an expense is growing above budget each month, say so; don't refer to a "decline in the rate of increase in the variance."

3. *Apply statistical techniques fairly.* Don't abandon one analysis because it doesn't support your hypothesis. Take the approach that you will first identify the problem and then find the most dependable answer. Statistical analysis is a useful and powerful tool if used properly.

Set standards for yourself, including the methods you will use in validating your raw data, in defining problems you will answer, and in presenting your facts. Don't allow yourself to use your knowledge of statistics to distort or manipulate, and apply the same rule to others in your department.

WORK PROJECT

1. You work for a professional corporation. The president has expressed concern about the rate of nonbillable hours (hours professionals are paid that cannot be charged to clients). You summarize the trend for the last six months:

Month	Hours Billed	Nonbillable Hours
Jan	419	39
Feb	483	47
Mar	462	44
Apr	574	57
May	492	51
Jun	521	53

a. What is the ratio of nonbillable hours each month to hours billed, expressed as a percentage?

b. What hypothesis might you develop in examining the trend in nonbillable hours?

2. Using the same information found in question 1, compute the following for nonbillable hours:

   a. Month-to-month change, using 40 hours as the index value, 100.

   b. Percentage of change from month to month.

   c. A three-month moving average, weighting the oldest month at 1, the middle month at 2, and the latest month at 3.

3. How would your analysis of trends in nonbillable hours be affected by:

   a. Increases in the number of professionals on the staff?

   b. The president's decision to begin holding one-hour weekly staff meetings?

   c. Installation of a new, more efficient computer system to track hours and prepare bills?

10

Information Sources

There are two kinds of statistics, the kind you look up and the kind you make up.

—Rex Stout

A meeting was called to review the results of a recent market sample for a new product. The president started out by asking, "Will we make a profit?"

The manager of the research department answered, "Based on the specific assumptions applied in our test, there is a reasonable likelihood that response will fall within our range of expectation."

The president leaned over and whispered to his secretary, "What was the answer?"

She whispered back, "Yes."

It's very hard for a statistician to give an absolute answer, because probabilities are never absolute. The best you can hope for is a "reasonable expectation."

That doesn't mean you can't use statistical techniques to make decisions, or that a probability study is worthless. As you saw in the last chapter, trying to answer a question may only make the question itself more complicated than you thought at first. The real value of statistical techniques is that they help you to narrow down the field of possible outcomes. Those most likely to occur can then be isolated and used for estimates of the future.

You may break down analysis into two categories. First is analysis of the past, the routines practiced in the field of accounting and book-keeping—recording and classifying transactions and then preparing financial statements. Second is analysis of the likely or possible future, which may include budgeting and forecasting, business planning, market planning, product testing, and all other questions dealing with the unknown outcome of future events.

Just as accountants gather information to prepare financial statements, you can gather raw data to help with the task of predicting probable future events. A financial statement is based on certainties—the actual transactions experienced during a period of time and the current value of assets and liabilities. These facts lead to absolute conclusions. The future, though, is not as clear. Business transactions depend on how a set of raw data is interpreted, the hypothesis applied to the situation, and the estimation of likelihood for one or more possible outcomes.

GATHERING YOUR RAW DATA

The process of gathering information for statistical work is similar to the process of recording entries in the books. The accountant needs to capture and record every transaction for income, costs, and expenses; to arrange and report their meaning; and to anticipate the future (through planning and budgeting). Thus, the accountant works from a well-understood set of raw data.

The task you face in accumulating raw data may involve much less certainty. First, you must decide what raw data are valid for the projections you are asked to make. Second, your role as interpreter is not as structured or widely understood as the accountant's role.

Example: You expect your company to automate the processing that takes place in your department within the next year. Accordingly, you begin keeping records of transaction load—time required to complete tasks, average number of transactions processed, exceptions to general procedures, probable levels of future transactions, and so forth.

Even with a very detailed file of raw data, you won't know whether or not it will help in answering questions likely to come up in the future—because you can't know how a problem will be addressed by someone else. For example, by keeping files on transactions, you assume that the method of automation will be based on a study of existing work load. But that doesn't ensure that it will be the approach actually taken, or that your recommendations based on transaction records will be considered valid in the decision-making process.

Here's a suggested approach to gathering raw data: Anticipate the questions likely to be asked in the future, the problems you expect to encounter. Then prepare accordingly. Part of your task in estimating the future involves anticipating methods for solving problems—assuming those problems are universal. These may include dealing with variances in expense accounts, hiring to avoid understaffing in the department, or changing service procedures to respond to customers during periods of sales expansion.

Another part of your job should deal with looking to the future to anticipate questions that haven't yet been asked. If you're able to perform this task well, you will be prepared to provide answers based on a body of facts, rather than having to do a lot of research under the pressure of deadline. You may need to overlook the possibility that your approach won't help and be ready to take a leading role in how the issue is addressed. In other words, gather your facts so that *your* solution simply makes sense.

Example: You have had problems budgeting accurately in the past because of incomplete assumptions about some elements of certain accounts. So this year, you begin keeping records detailing what goes into the accounts you've had problems with in the past. When your next budget is prepared, you use your raw data file to prepare a more complete estimate of future expenses.

Example: Operating procedures are being changed in your department. You also expect to need more employees within six months because management is forecasting a big increase in sales volume. You start a file to record the time required for major tasks under the new procedure so that you will be able to support the expected request for a bigger payroll budget later on.

Outside Sources

The information you compile today may come from a source outside your department. For example, a marketing director gives information concerning recruitment, contact activity, and average volume to the accounting department; accounting prepares a forecast and sends it back to marketing. The exchange of information goes on constantly.

The same type of activity can take place between any two departments, divisions, subsidiaries, or sections. Exchanges of information can also occur between you and people outside the company.

Example: You are preparing a section of the current year's business plan involving expenses in a new region. You contact suppliers and ask for current prices on a range of supplies and materials.

Example: You are working on a budget for the treasurer's office. During the next year, management plans to seek a loan for $50,000. You call the company's bank to find out the probable interest rate and monthly payments.

In each instance, an outside source was contacted and asked to supply raw data. But could an estimate be done more accurately, or more scientifically, by building a file of raw data that is more comprehensive?

Example: In contacting suppliers in a newly developed region to estimate levels of expenses and costs, it may not be enough to gather quotations on what's being charged today. If your budget extends a full year, these steps may make the information more complete:

- Ask each supplier whether a price increase is anticipated during the next 12 months.
- Ask for the last date a price increase was put into effect.
- Ask whether prices are reduced for volume purchases, or if discounts are allowed for timely payment.
- Compare buying patterns and past variances in existing regions of similar size and budget. Base your budget estimates partly on historical records.

Example: Besides checking with the bank your company usually uses for financing, what about finding out the rates charged for similar loans by other institutions? What trends have been established in the last three years? Do rates vary for shorter-term and longer-term loans? Can you figure out an amortization schedule without consulting the bank?

Outside information should be validated and qualified. Just because a supplier currently charges a specified amount for a part, it doesn't mean that price will be offered next year, or even next week. In fact, unless you ask, you may not even know whether the supplier will continue to offer that part. And a bank will not guarantee a loan rate for very long, if at all. Those policies change with the cost of money from the institution's point of view.

Internal Sources

A second source for information is your own department. Many aspects of the issues affecting your future can be estimated from what you have at hand. An informed response to issues imposed from the outside often depends on the facts you can document.

Example: You are responsible for tracking and processing a large volume of transactions, and the volume has been rising during the last two years. Your company's budget committee has recommended against approval of your request for two additional employees in the coming year. The raw data you've accumulated in anticipation of resistance to your request show that your staff size has not grown at all for 24 months; but today, employees are handling an average of 40 percent more transactions. Management is forecasting more growth next year. Your information supports your position, and your budget is approved.

Example: During a series of meetings, a debate has taken place as to whether or not your company should expand to a new region. You kept careful records of historical cost and expense levels during the last expansion phase, and you use those to estimate probabilities of success for the new plan. This does not answer the broader question of whether or not the timing is right; but it does better define the issues, identify the risk level, and clarify the entire discussion for everyone involved.

CREATING THE SOURCE FILE

To gather useful, meaningful raw data, you do not need to anticipate specific problems that can't possibly be known at present. As a manager, you already understand the issues that affect your department and your company. The accounting department may be an excellent source for financial information, and the payroll department can supply you with data on employment. In addition, you already know the types of information you need to keep for the future. They may include statistics on employee performance, transaction processing, accuracy and error rates, costs and expenses, sales, customer inquiries, and other matters you can track. You may develop and follow your own trends and work up meaningful ratios as a control tool as well as for use as raw data in the future.

Your data file does not have to take up a great deal of file space, and it shouldn't demand a lot of your time. Spending a few minutes per day or a few hours per month, you can accumulate a lot of useful information.

Example: Management insists that all employees keep files on task procedures. Each time a task changes, you're supposed to make sure a revised procedure is written. You want to make a recommendation that the task-procedure requirement be dropped, because you believe it costs the company an excessive amount of money. You keep track of the time required to keep manuals up-to-date in your department over a six-month period. Your study reveals that the average employee in the department spends three hours per month on updating or writing task descriptions. After six months of observation, you prepare your recommendation report, expressing the time your employees spend on updating manuals in terms of total cost. You estimate the cost to the entire company of 812 nonmanagement employees by using your 12-person department as a sample.

For this study, internal information (from the department) was used as the sample for your conclusion. The financial result was supported by outside information (the number of nonmanagement employees and the average hourly rate they are paid, supplied by the personnel department). Your findings show the following:

If every nonmanagement employee devotes three hours per month to maintaining task procedures, the cost per month to the company is:

Number of Employees	812
Average hourly wage	$12.60
Cost per hour	$10,231.20
Hours spent per month	3
Total monthly cost	$30,693.60

Your conclusion, that the company is currently spending in excess of $30,000 per month to maintain task-procedure descriptions, assumes that all departments keep their manuals up-to-date and that your department is typical. This information can be compared with the average cost of training new employees when no existing task descriptions exist.

The thorough gathering of information can provide you with the facts needed to support a recommendation you make for changes in procedure, especially when your sample proves that the expense of a current procedure or policy is excessively high. That's putting raw data to good use.

IMPROVING COMMUNICATION

Using statistical information correctly will improve your ability to communicate within the company. Referring to the previous example, consider how you might suggest dropping the procedure without facts to back up the idea.

Without a statistical procedure to back up your idea, the typical arguments you could make include:

It takes too much time.

No one keeps the task descriptions up-to-date anyway, so what good are they?

I end up training new employees from scratch. The descriptions usually aren't any help.
No one likes having to do it.

None of these arguments will help your case, and none of them indicate good reasons to abandon the procedure. All the statements may even be true. But management will respond better to proof. Accumulating the information to support what you believe won't take a lot of time, and it won't be too complex to interpret.

The report in the example assumed that every nonmanagement employee in the company spent three hours per month working on updating task procedures. But what if you make the presentation and someone challenges the assumption, saying they believe it's too high?

If you've done your statistical work thoroughly, you will be able to answer the challenge to your conclusion with facts, such as:

Management estimated the average monthly time required would run at four hours per employee; so this estimate may even be low.
Even if the estimate is cut in half, our monthly cost is still over $15,000.
What's a more realistic number, and how can you support it?

The point is that no one else will have undertaken the study, so no one else will have any better information on which to base a challenge. You're at an advantage because your conclusion is developed with facts. This approach does improve your communication skills, taking you away from the broad, unsupported *belief* and moving you closer to the scientifically developed conclusion. Remember: A SCIENTIFICALLY, METHODICALLY DEVELOPED CONCLUSION IS MORE CREDIBLE THAN MERE OPINION, EVEN WHEN BASED ON ASSUMPTIONS AND ESTIMATES.

Applying knowledge of statistics to a problem doesn't mean you have to train others so that they understand your procedures. You certainly won't want to expose a conference room full of fellow managers to your worksheets and calculations, expecting them to comprehend your regression analysis formula or variance study. Good communication is simple and direct. State the conclusion and make recommendations. Then, when you're questioned or challenged, be prepared to back up your report with the level of detail the challenge requires. Your response may occur on several levels:

Level 1. An explanation of your hypothesis and the procedure used to conduct a study. (In the example, the hypothesis was that the task-procedure description is excessively expensive. The procedure was to study the time spent on that activity in your department over a six-month period and to estimate the cost for the whole company on the basis of average wages paid to nonmanagement personnel.)

Level 2. Presentation of raw data developed internally as well as externally. (In the example, this includes a summary of your internal study and the facts personnel sent to you.)

Level 3. Detailed analysis. (In the example, this includes your worksheets for the hours each employee spent on task-description updating, those for any mathematical formulating, and those used to determine average costs incurred by the sample.)

STATISTICS AND YOUR CAREER

The issues you will confront in your career may come from the outside or from your own efforts. Outside issues include questions of budgeting and forecasting, market and business planning, expansion of products and services, and attempts to expand business influence and competitive position.

Inside issues, those stemming from your own efforts, include recommendations to management that will improve marketing or operational procedures, save money, or improve customer service. These ideas may be as simple as hiring a new employee or buying a piece of equipment, or as complex as moving into a new market, opening branch offices, or risking thousands of dollars in a new promotional effort.

All these issues involve decisions, and if the wrong decision is made, the company risks a loss. The perception may be that your career path depends largely on the point of view you express and on the ideas you communicate to management. In other words, if you're wrong, your career could be in jeopardy. Whether that is true or just perceived to be true, the chance you take in offering ideas will be reduced once you are able to define risk and narrow down the field of possible outcomes for your ideas.

Statistical techniques won't give you all the answers. And they won't ensure that your budgets and estimates will be any more accurate than they would be without applying a specific formula. These techniques should be counted among the tools you have available to evaluate and judge the future better. That's a big part of your job. In describing what they do for a living, many people talk about the daily routines— processing transactions, selling products and services, recording information, solving customer problems, or gathering information used by another department. What's rarely mentioned is "predicting or estimating the future."

The statistician is often described as someone unable to give a yes or no answer. Every response may be prefaced with "that depends . . ." or with "our limited study indicated. . . ." As frustrating as it is to get a qualified answer, the uncertainty is understandable. But as a manager, you can gain from statistical techniques that can give you the knowledge and focus to suggest a solution, offer a plan, or propose a budget with confidence, both in the numbers and in yourself.

WORK PROJECT

1. You are putting together a report proposing that your payroll budget be increased by two additional employees. Your reasoning: According to management's current sales forecast, you will be receiving a lot more work in the coming year than you have now. Name three possible sources for statistical support of your proposal.
2. You're part of a project team put together to study an out-of-state region into which your company wants to expand. Your job is to estimate payroll costs your company would incur. Name three outside sources worth checking.
3. Your company is about to offer a new product to the market. In evaluating the test area under consideration, name three factors you should check to make sure the area is representative of your overall market.

Appendix
Work Project Answers

CHAPTER 1

1. Isolating a representative grouping from a larger body of information is an efficient and necessary way to perform analysis. This is a basic premise of statistics. Answers to the three-part question are:
    a. The small group isolated for study is called a sample.
    b. The larger body of information is referred to as the population.
    c. The study described will *not* be accurate if new training procedures have been installed. Because the purpose of the study is to estimate future training requirements, a study based on the past cannot be used.
2. Before deciding how to respond to a request, you must first understand what is needed; you must understand the problem in order to solve it:
    a. Gathering facts will suffice in many cases. As long as a request is for information alone, this is the most direct response.
    b. Facts may also be arranged in a sequence that addresses the question. For example, if another department wants to know the most profitable division, a report should show divisions in order of profitability.
    c. In many cases, it is necessary to ask for clarification before responding. When a request is made for more information, the order of presentation may be affected, depending on what the other person or department needs to achieve.
3. A coin flip is a well-understood example of statistics as well as probability. Because there are only two possible outcomes, we know

that every flip has a 50 percent probability of landing on each side. In a review of a past series of coin flips, it is also possible to establish statistical outcomes. If a coin is flipped enough times, it can be statistically proved that each outcome has a 50 percent chance of occurring. Probability is the prediction of results when the process is understood; statistics is a study of outcomes when the process is not known.

CHAPTER 2

1. The mean, median, and mode are the three tests of central tendency:
   a. The mean, or average, is calculated by adding the values and then dividing by the number of values. The total of the nine months' customer complaints is 1,363:

$$\frac{1,363}{9} = 151.4$$

   b. The median is the value in the exact middle of the list; half the values are larger, and half are smaller than the median. Arrange the list in value order:

   1. 207
   2. 193
   3. 193
   4. 188
   5. 174
   6. 122
   7. 106
   8. 92
   9. 88

   The median is the fifth value, 174.
   c. The mode is the value that appears most frequently. If no value appears more than once, there is no mode. In this example, the value 193 appears twice; that is the mode.

2. The dispersion factor is calculated by one of two methods, mean absolute value or variance. Begin by putting the available information in a table:

Number	Mean	Distance	Square
35	34	1	1
26	34	8	64
19	34	15	225
45	34	11	121
42	34	8	64
37	34	3	9
			484

a. The mean absolute deviation is calculated by adding the square of the distance between each value and the mean and then dividing the total by the number of values:

$$\frac{1 + 64 + 225 + 121 + 64 + 9}{6} = 80.7$$

b. The variance is calculated by squaring each value and dividing the total by the number of values, then subtracting the square of the mean.

Step 1:

$$\frac{35^2 + 26^2 + 19^2 + 45^2 + 42^2 + 37^2}{6} = 1,236.7$$

Step 2:

$$1,236.7 - 34^2$$
$$= 1,236.7 - 1,156$$
$$= 80.7$$

3. The answer to number 2b above is a factor that represents the square of the number of sales calls. This by itself does not tell you how to measure dispersion, either by the average number of calls whose values vary from the mean, or by the percentage of variance. To derive these totals:

a. The standard deviation is calculated by finding the square root of the dispersion factor (the number that, when multiplied by itself, produces the dispersion factor). In this case, it is 8.98 sales calls.

b. The coefficient of variation is a measure of the percentage of dispersion. It is calculated by dividing the standard deviation by the mean:

$$\frac{8.98}{34} = 26.4\%$$

CHAPTER 3

1. Proper construction of a graph begins with careful planning of the scale. Your goal should be to build a graph that accurately represents the trend or status within a comfortable, well-balanced space.

a. The time span is six months and the value range extends up to 12,615 transactions. The best balance will be achieved by setting the top-to-bottom (value) in 2,000-transaction units. An alternative would be to use 1,000-transaction units and increase the spacing of the left-to-right timeline.

b. A graph based on percent increase would use these figures:

Month	Number	Percentage
Jan	6,215	–
Feb	9,411	151
Mar	4,678	50
Apr	3,009	64
May	12,615	419
Jun	8,451	67

This method would make the graph inaccurate because the percent increase or decrease from one month to another does not reveal the trend. The purpose should be to estimate average monthly transaction levels, but the percentage by which that level changes each month will be distorted when transaction levels are exceptionally high or low.

c. An indexed graph based on the assumption that the first month's transaction level represents 100 would use these figures:

Month	Number	Percentage
Jan	6,215	100
Feb	9,411	151
Mar	4,678	75
Apr	3,009	48
May	12,615	203
Jun	8,451	136

This variation of indexing is more stable than the previous one because the statistics for months two through five are based on the same starting point. However, the problem with this alternative is that the transaction level for January may not be representative of a typical month. Unless you are able to validate January's level as an acceptable norm, indexing would not necessarily result in an accurate trend.

2. The purpose of this graph is to show the history of accidents that occurred during a one-year period. The range of occurrences presents a scaling problem because of the distorted November figure.

a. The division is inaccurate. The first 8 units are separated by 5, and the last has a gap of 45. Scaling should always be consistent.

b. The best scaling for this assignment would have units of 10 (9 segments from zero to 90) or 8 (11 units from zero to 88). That would make the graph approximately square or slightly rectangular.

c. Because the trend is a negative occurrence, it might be effective to reverse the value scale. Start with zero at the top and increase the count downward.

3. A circle graph is built in two steps. First, the values are converted to

percentages of the whole, totaling 100 percent; second, the percentages are converted to degrees of the circle, totaling 360 degrees. To compute step 1, divide the hours for each of the activities by 40.0:

Activity	Hours	Percentage
Recurring routines	16.3	40.7
Meetings	3.0	7.5
Problem solving	9.4	23.5
Discussions with others	1.6	4.0
Discussions with boss	0.6	1.5
Coffee breaks	0.5	1.3
Idle time	8.6	21.5
Total	40.0	100.0

To compute step 2, multiply each percentage by 360°. (For example, express 40.7 percent in decimal form, or .407, and multiply by 360°.) Then round to the nearest full degree:

Activity	Percentage					Degrees
Recurring routines	40.7	×	360	=		147
Meetings	7.5	×	360	=		27
Problem solving	23.5	×	360	=		85
Discussions with others	4.0	×	360	=		14
Discussions with boss	1.5	×	360	=		5
Coffee breaks	1.3	×	360	=		5
Idle time	21.5	×	360	=		77
Total	100.0					360

The degrees are then computed on a circle with a protractor starting from a base line. When all the activity segments have been calculated, the entire circle will be used up.

CHAPTER 4

1. To develop a list of possible outcomes, remember two points: First, it is possible that two or more of the new sales regions could have

identical results, and second, because the sequence is not important, you want to avoid duplicates. For example, a 1-2-4 outcome counts the same as a 4-1-2 outcome. The purpose of this exercise is to identify the probability that a particular range group will result within a particular region. Mathematical values are assigned to the range groups so that a statistical summary of these probabilities is possible. Build your list in numerical order:

1 and 1 and 1	1 and 4 and 4	2 and 5 and 5
1 and 1 and 2	1 and 4 and 5	3 and 3 and 3
1 and 1 and 3	1 and 5 and 5	3 and 3 and 4
1 and 1 and 4	2 and 2 and 2	3 and 3 and 5
1 and 1 and 5	2 and 2 and 3	3 and 4 and 4
1 and 2 and 2	2 and 2 and 4	3 and 4 and 5
1 and 2 and 3	2 and 2 and 5	3 and 5 and 5
1 and 2 and 4	2 and 3 and 3	4 and 4 and 4
1 and 2 and 5	2 and 3 and 4	4 and 4 and 5
1 and 3 and 3	2 and 3 and 5	4 and 5 and 5
1 and 3 and 4	2 and 4 and 4	5 and 5 and 5
1 and 3 and 5	2 and 4 and 5	

There are 35 possible outcomes in the three regions collectively.

2. Once a mathematical list has been compiled, it is next divided into sequence by total count. For example, the total count for the first combination (1-1-1) is 3; and the count for the last combination (5-5-5) is 15:

1-1-1	3	1-3-4	8	1-5-5	11
1-1-2	4	2-2-4	8	2-4-5	11
1-1-3	5	2-3-3	8	3-3-5	11
1-2-2	5	1-3-5	9	3-4-4	11
1-1-4	6	1-4-4	9	2-5-5	12
1-2-3	6	2-2-5	9	3-4-5	12
2-2-2	6	2-3-4	9	4-4-4	12
1-1-5	7	3-3-3	9	3-5-5	13
1-2-4	7	1-4-5	10	4-4-5	13
1-3-3	7	2-3-5	10	4-5-5	14
2-2-3	7	2-4-4	10	5-5-5	15
1-2-5	8	3-3-4	10		

3. By dividing the list into likely outcomes, you narrow down the probability. Those mathematical results that occur most frequently have a greater likelihood of occurring.

a. You know there are 35 possible outcomes. First divide the list developed in question 2 into the groups corresponding to the 5 outcome groups:

Group	Results
1	3 and 4
2	5 and 6 and 7
3	8 and 9 and 10
4	11 and 12 and 13
5	14 and 15

Next, count the number of chances in each group and divide by the total, 35:

Outcome	Number of Chances	Percentage
1	2	5.7
2	9	25.7
3	13	37.2
4	9	25.7
5	2	5.7
Total	35	100.0

A report on the probabilities can now state:

Recruitment Level	Percent Chance
90 to 99	37.2
80 to 89	25.7
100 to 109	25.7
70 to 79	5.7
110 to 119	5.7

b. The report can be simplified even more by doing away with the least likely outcomes, represented by outcome ranges 1 and 5. The percent breakdown can now be explained on the basis of 31 possible results:

Group	Results
2	5 and 6 and 7
3	8 and 9 and 10
4	11 and 12 and 13

Counting the outcomes in these groups and expressing them in percentages, we get the following:

Outcome	Number of Chances	Percentage
2	9	29.0
3	13	42.0
4	9	29.0
Total	31	100.0

The report on the probabilities now states:

Recruitment Level	Percent Chance
90 to 99	42
80 to 89	29
100 to 109	29

CHAPTER 5

1. This exercise helps you to define the degree of variation, which allows you to compare one series of values with the relative variation in another.

a. Add and square the four values:

$$\frac{37^2 + 46^2 + 29^2 + 26^2}{4} + 1{,}250.5$$

b. First compute the square of the mean. The mean, or average, of the values is:

$$\frac{37 + 46 + 29 + 26}{4} + 34.5$$

The square of the mean is:

$$34.5^2 = 1{,}190.25$$

Subtract the square of the mean from the answer to item a above:

Answer to item a	1,250.5
Less	1,190.25
	60.25

c. The square root of the answer to item b above is:

$$\sqrt{60.25} = 7.76$$

d. Divide the answer to item c above by the mean:

$$\frac{7.76}{34.5} = 22.5$$

e. The square root of the answer to item b above (step c) is the number of hours of variance. The answer is 7.76 hours.
f. Step d gives the percentage and is called the coefficient of variation. The answer is 22.5 percent.
2. The purpose of figuring out permutations and combinations is to identify the range of possible outcomes. With that information in

hand, you will be able to isolate a limited range of outcomes and compute the percentage that it represents.

a. To perform permutations and combinations, you will first need to compute factorials, which represent multiplications of every whole number between 1 and the subject number:

Transactions
$$8! = 1 \times 2 \times 3 \times 4 \times 5 \times 6 \times 7 \times 8$$
$$= 40,320$$

$$5! = 1 \times 2 \times 3 \times 4 \times 5$$
$$= 120$$

Project Team
$$9! = 1 \times 2 \times 3 \times 4 \times 5 \times 6 \times 7 \times 8 \times 9$$
$$= 362,880$$

$$3! = 1 \times 2 \times 3$$
$$= 6$$

Job Openings
$$7! = 1 \times 2 \times 3 \times 4 \times 5 \times 6 \times 7$$
$$= 5,040$$

$$6! = 1 \times 2 \times 3 \times 4 \times 5 \times 6$$
$$= 720$$

b. Permutations are calculated using the factorials of factors (n) and arrangements (r):

Transactions

$$^{8}P_5 = \frac{8!}{(8-5)!}$$

$$= \frac{40,320}{6}$$

$$= 6,720$$

Project Team

$$^9P_3 = \frac{9!}{(9-3)!}$$

$$= \frac{362,880}{720}$$

$$= 504$$

Job Openings

$$^7P_6 = \frac{7!}{(7-6)!}$$

$$= \frac{5,040}{1}$$

$$= 5,040$$

c. There will be fewer combinations for the same factors and arrangements because reverse-order outcomes are not counted:

Transactions

$$^8C_5 = \frac{8!}{5!(8-5)!}$$

$$= \frac{40,320}{120 \times 6}$$

$$= 56$$

Project Team

$$^9C_3 = \frac{9!}{3!(9-3)!}$$

$$= \frac{362,880}{6 \times 720}$$

$$= 84$$

Job Openings

$$^7C_6 = \frac{7!}{6!(7-6)!}$$

$$= \frac{5,040}{720 \times 1}$$

$$= 7$$

3. To develop a weighted average, multiply each period's value by the weighting factor. Then divide the accumulated totals for each period by the weighting values to the same period. For example, the March total is the sum of the totals for January, February, and March (103 + 236 + 327, or 666); the weighting factor is the sum of weight assigned to that point (1 + 2 + 3, or 6). Weighted average is 666 divided by 6, or 111.

Month	Calls	Weight	Total	Weighted Average
Jan	103	1	103	103
Feb	118	2	236	113
Mar	109	3	327	111
Apr	126	4	504	117
May	182	5	910	139
Jun	121	6	726	134
Jul	133	7	931	133
Aug	172	8	1,376	142
Sep	113	9	1,017	136
Oct	155	10	1,550	140
Nov	162	11	1,782	143
Dec	149	12	1,788	144
Total	1643		11,250	

CHAPTER 6

1. The factorial expression is an abbreviation for the combination formula. That formula's bottom half consists of the bottom value's

factorial multiplied by the factorial of the difference between the top
and bottom numbers.

a. The combination formulas are:

(1) $\dbinom{10}{6} = \dfrac{10!}{6!(10-6)!}$

(2) $\dbinom{9}{4} = \dfrac{9!}{4!(9-4)!}$

(3) $\dbinom{7}{2} = \dfrac{7!}{2!(7-2)!}$

b. The factorial expressions are:

(1) $\dfrac{6!}{2!(6-2)!} = \dbinom{6}{2}$

(2) $\dfrac{11!}{7!(11-7)!} = \dbinom{11}{7}$

(3) $\dfrac{8!}{2!(8-2)!} = \dbinom{8}{2}$

2. The binomial distribution contains three separate parts: the computation of possible combinations; the probability of the successful
result; and the probability of remaining results.

a. $\Pr(x=6) = \dbinom{9}{6} .65^6 (1-.65)^{9-6}$

$= \left(\dfrac{362,880}{720(6)}\right) .07542 \,(.35)^3$

$= 84 \times .07542 \times .04287$

$= .272$

b. $\Pr(x=7) = \dbinom{10}{7} .80^7 (1-.80)^{10-7}$

$= \dfrac{3,628,800}{5,040(6)} .20972 \, (.20)^3$

$= 120 \times .20972 \times .00800$

$= .201$

c. $\Pr(x=6) = \dbinom{11}{6} .45^6 (1-.45)^{11-6}$

$= \left(\dfrac{39,916,800}{720(120)}\right) .00830 \, (.55)^5$

$= 462 \times .00830 \times .05033$

$= .193$

3. A hypergeometric distribution is a series of combinations. Combinations of possible successes are multiplied by combinations of other outcomes, and the result is divided by the total possible combinations:

a. $\Pr(x=3) = \dfrac{\dbinom{4}{3} \; \dbinom{3}{2}}{\dbinom{7}{5}}$

$= \dfrac{\left(\dfrac{24}{6(1)}\right) \; \left(\dfrac{6}{2(1)}\right)}{\dfrac{5,040}{120\,(2)}}$

$= \dfrac{(4) \;\; (3)}{21}$

$= \dfrac{12}{21}$

$= 57.1\%$

b. $\Pr(x=2) = \dfrac{\dbinom{6}{2}\dbinom{4}{1}}{\dbinom{10}{3}}$

$= \dfrac{\left(\dfrac{720}{2(24)}\right)\left(\dfrac{24}{1(6)}\right)}{\dfrac{3,628,800}{6(5,040)}}$

$= \dfrac{(15)\ \ (4)}{120}$

$= \dfrac{60}{120}$

$= 50.0\%$

c. $\Pr(x=3) = \dfrac{\dbinom{5}{3}\dbinom{3}{1}}{\dbinom{8}{4}}$

$= \dfrac{\left(\dfrac{120}{6\,(2)}\right)\left(\dfrac{6}{1(2)}\right)}{\dfrac{40,320}{24(24)}}$

$= \dfrac{(10)\ \ (3)}{70}$

$= \dfrac{30}{70}$

$= 42.9\%$

CHAPTER 7

1. The fixed monthly fee of $8.00 is unchanging, no matter how many or how few checks you write. That amount is the value of coefficient *a*. The 15¢ per check charge is coefficient *b*. The regression line formula identifies the value of the dependent variable *Y*, which is based on changing values in the independent variable *X* (number of checks). In each calculation, the value of coefficient *a* will be 8.00 and the value of coefficient *b* will be .15. The formula is:

$$Y = a + bX$$

a. $Y = 8.00 + .15(150)$
   $= \$30.50$

b. $Y = 8.00 + .15(225)$
   $= \$41.75$

c. $Y = 8.00 + .15(300)$
   $= \$53.00$

2. The table is built completely from the known values of *X* (number of people on the payroll for the last year) and *Y* (selling expenses, in hundreds). The other columns are constructed in the following ways:

x: the distance from the mean of *X*. For example, 42 (January) minus the mean of 44 equals -2. And 46 (April) minus the mean of 44 equals $+2$.

y: the distance from the mean of *Y*. For example, 129 (January) minus the mean of 130 equals -1. And 132 (April) minus the mean of 130 equals $+2$.

x^2: the value of *x* squared. For example, the January *x* value, -2, when squared equals 4. The squared values are all listed as positives, without regard for the sign of the values before they are squared. The interest here is the degree of squared deviation from the mean, not the direction of deviation.

y^2: the value of *y* squared. For example, the March *y* value, -4, when squared equals 16. As in the previous column, it doesn't matter whether the answer is a plus or minus; the degree matters, the direction of deviation does not.

xy: values in column *x* multiplied by values in column y.

a. The completed table is:

Month	X	Y	x	y	x^2	y^2	xy
Jan	42	$129	−2	−1	4	1	2
Feb	43	130	−1	0	1	0	0
Mar	41	126	−3	−4	9	16	12
Apr	46	132	2	2	4	4	4
May	44	130	0	0	0	0	0
Jun	48	133	4	3	16	9	12
Total	264	$780	0	0	34	30	30
Mean	44	$130					

b. When the least squares are computed, the values of coefficients *b* and *a* are worked out with the formulas:

$$b = \frac{xy}{x^2} \qquad a = \frac{Y - (Xb)}{n}$$

From the table in item a, the following values are needed for these computations:

$xy = 30$
$x^2 = 34$
$Y = 780$
$X = 264$
$n = 6$ (number of months)

Substituting these values into the formulas, we have:

$$b = \frac{30}{34}$$

$$= .8824$$

$$a = \frac{780 - (264 \times .8824)}{6}$$

$$= \frac{780 - 232.95}{6}$$

$$= 91.175$$

3. With coefficients *a* and *b* known, the least-squares calculation of a regression line depends on the same formula used before:

$$Y = a + bX$$

This is applied to each case, remembering that the answers must be converted from hundreds of dollars to actual dollars.

a. $Y = 91.175 + (.8824 \times 50)$
    $= 135.30$ ($13,530)

b. $Y = 91.175 + (.8824 \times 55)$
    $= 139.71$ ($13,971)

c. $Y = 91.175 + (.8824 \times 60)$
    $= 144.12$ ($14,412)

CHAPTER 8

1. The purpose of this exercise is to isolate the degree of chi-square variance. That requires a comparison between expected and actual.
   a. The null hypothesis is that preferences in all regions will conform to overall test results. Collectively, 497 people chose product 1, or 50.2 percent of those tested. And 493 chose product 2, or 49.8 percent of those tested.
   b. Expectation values are:

Region A, product 1: 50.2% of 520, or 261
Region B, product 1: 50.2% of 470, or 236
Region A, product 2: 49.8% of 520, or 259
Region B, product 2: 49.8% of 470, or 234
Total   990

c. The first column of the worksheet lists the expected outcome, and the second shows the actual. The difference between column 1 and column 2 (column 3) is squared (column 4), and the square is divided by expected outcome to arrive at chi-square (column 5). The totals in column 5 are then added:

Expected Outcome	Actual Outcome	Difference	Difference	Chi-Square
261	241	20	400	1.53
236	256	−20	400	1.69
259	279	−20	400	1.54
234	214	20	400	1.71
				6.47

d. Chi-square can be arrived at using the formula given in the chapter, which is nothing more than a different version of the table in item c above:

$$= \frac{(261-241)^2}{261} + \frac{(236-256)^2}{236} + \frac{(259-279)^2}{259} + \frac{(234-214)^2}{234}$$

$$= \frac{400}{261} + \frac{400}{236} + \frac{400}{259} + \frac{400}{234}$$

$$= 1.53 + 1.69 + 1.54 + 1.71$$

$$= 6.47$$

2. In order to determine the significance of 6.47 (the answer to question 1), you will need to compare that result to the chi-square distribution tables.

a. There are two degrees of freedom, one for each region. If you count products tested, instead of regions, the same result is achieved.

b. The chi-square distribution table (Table 3) shows that for two degrees of freedom and an assumed significance level of 10 percent (.10), the maximum expected variation will be 4.6.

   c. Chi-square variation is 6.47 in the example, but Table 3 reveals that in 90 percent of cases (100 percent less 10 percent), variation will be less than 4.6. This is a significant variation.* Therefore, product preference is different in the two regions tested.
3. Standard error of difference identifies the amount of variance by which a sample is expected to deviate from the average.
   a. The formula (Figure 8-2) is:

$$S = \sqrt{\frac{A(100-A)}{n} + \frac{B(100-B)}{n}}$$

$$= \sqrt{\frac{31(100-31)}{200} + \frac{35(100-35)}{200}}$$

$$= \sqrt{\frac{31 \times 69}{200} + \frac{35 \times 65}{200}}$$

$$= \sqrt{10{,}695 + 11.375}$$

$$= \sqrt{22.07}$$

$$= 4.70$$

   b. The deviation in the example is not significant. It is only 4 percent (35 less 31). But the standard error of difference reveals that you may expect deviation at or below 4.7 percent.

CHAPTER 9

1. The statistics compiled reveal that there is a close relationship between hours billed and nonbillable hours. This will help in analysis and in starting out with a reasonable hypothesis.
   a. Compute the ratio by dividing nonbillable hours by hours billed. For example, the January answer is:

---

*The chi-square, 6.47, is greater than the indicated standard of 4.6 or below.

$$\frac{39}{419} = 9.3\%$$

Applying the same formula to the other five months, we have:

Feb	9.7%
Mar	9.5
Apr	9.9
May	10.4
Jun	10.2

b. When the percentage of one set of numbers is compared to the other, the direction and degree of change can be observed. A reasonable hypothesis would be that the percentage of nonbillable hours will rise in direct relationship to the volume of hours billed.

2. There are a number of ways that nonbillable hours could be expressed for graphic presentation, statistical analysis, or a probability study.

a. An index is a way of expressing numerical information on the assumption that a particular value is the starting point, or 100 percent. All other values are then pegged to it. Divide each month's value by 40 (index value of 100) to find its index value:

Jan	39/40 =	97.5
Feb	47/40 =	117.5
Mar	44/40 =	110.0
Apr	57/40 =	142.5
May	51/40 =	127.5
Jun	53/40 =	132.5

b. Percentage of change is computed by dividing each month's result by the previous month's. In this exercise, the first month has no change in value, because it cannot be compared to a previous month:

Jan	39/ 0 =	– %
Feb	47/39 =	120.5
Mar	44/47 =	93.6
Apr	57/44 =	129.5

May   51/57 =   89.5
Jun   53/51 = 103.9

c. A weighted average is one in which later values are given more weight than earlier ones. A three-month moving average with weighting of 1, 2, and 3 is computed by adding up weighted values, then dividing by the total weight value, 6:

Mar $39 \times 1 = $ 39
          $47 \times 2 = $ 94
          $44 \times 3 = $ 132
         Total   265/6 = 44.2

Apr $47 \times 1 = $ 47
          $44 \times 2 = $ 88
          $57 \times 3 = $ 171
         Total   306/6 = 51.0

May $44 \times 1 = $ 44
          $57 \times 2 = $ 114
          $51 \times 3 = $ 153
         Total   311/6 = 51.8

Jun $57 \times 1 = $ 57
          $51 \times 2 = $ 102
          $53 \times 3 = $ 159
         Total   318/6 = 53.0

3. Considerations beyond what the numbers show should be taken into account when those factors change the environment, or invalidate past information.

a. If professional staff is being increased, it probably has an effect on the degree of nonbillable hours. To test that hypothesis, review historical information if available; or estimate the effect by reviewing changes in administrative procedures. It is a certainty that more people (meaning more hours billed) must also be expected to increase the level of nonbillable hours.

b. If all staff members will spend an additional hour per week in a nonbillable routine, the historical information must be altered to reflect that change, or not be used at all. For example, over 4.3 weeks per month, five staff members' nonbillable hours will grow by a monthly level of 21.5 hours.

c. A new system could affect the historical record. If efficiency has been increased, your hypothesis should allow for the possibility that today's record is more accurate than historical information.

CHAPTER 10

1. This is an example of a report generated not from the outside, but from your own initiative. Thus, the question is one you define for yourself. Your hypothesis is that the level of sales management as forecast will have a direct impact on your department and on its ability to perform. With that in mind, you will need to gather statistical facts to support your idea. These may include:

   a. A study of the work load in your department over a period of time. If you discover that the average employee is handling more work now than in the past, that supports your hypothesis.

   b. The sales forecast itself. If you tie your estimate of future work load to management's own numbers, that strengthens your contention.

   c. Changes in work load during previous expansion phases. If you can draw a correlation between previous-year changes in volume and corresponding work load, you may prove your point.

2. Consider checking these sources:

   a. Employment statistics in the state and, particularly, in the region under study. These should include salary levels as well as supply and demand trends. A state employment agency may be the best source; also check with employment agencies.

   b. Salaries paid by the competition, as well as the range of benefits offered.

   c. Applicable state and local payroll taxes, workers' compensation rates, and other costs of payroll.

3. The purpose is to ensure that the test market is as representative as

you have assumed. These are among the possible sources to confirm this hypothesis:

a. Buying trends for existing products offered in the region in comparison with patterns experienced in the overall market.
b. Recent developments in the economy of the area, such as population changes or changes in unemployment statistics.
c. Recent changes by your direct competition in the same area, including a comparison between their prices and the price you have in mind for your new product.

Index